TO
FREEDOM
AND BEYOND

TYNDALL

Every effort has been made to trace and contact owners of the paintings reproduced
in this book. The publishers apologize to those whom they have not been able to
approach for copyright permission and will be pleased to hear from them.

First United States Publication 1976
ABNER SCHRAM
ISBN 0-8390-0166-5
Library of Congress Catalog Number 74-29479

ISBN 85949 059 9

Printed and bound in Spain by
Novograph S.A. and Roner S.A., Madrid
D.L.: M 37360/1975

TO FREEDOM AND BEYOND

The development of French 19th-century painting ~ John Alabone

"Une œuvre d'art est un coin
de la création vu à travers un tempérament"
Émile Zola

"It is futile to assign the place an
artist is likely to take in the future. There are
fashions in immortality and there
are trivial fashions. . . . Books and pictures read
differently to different generations"
William Rothenstein

CONTENTS

LIST OF COLOUR PLATES

COMPLETE LIST OF WORKS ILLUSTRATED

With the outbreak of the Revolution in France in 1789 the fashionable world of *Versailles** came to an end. Symbolic of the new ideals, the decadence of pursued pleasure became outmoded. The art world, too, took up the challenge of revolution. Seldom in the history of art can the destiny of one man have been clearer; *Jacques Louis David* not only reflected the new *Jacobin* doctrines in his work but, also, his classical interest and archaeological knowledge enabled him to shape, in art form, the new images of authority.

Beset on all sides by enemies, the *New Republic* was urgently in need of spiritual inspiration. David manifested the new requirements of duty, sacrifice and total commitment to the State, in his numerous paintings. However, no matter how revolutionary his theories, his stylistic approach is rational and well ordered. To him, posterity owes the disciplines and intellectual approach to art, synonymous with the emergence of the *neo-classical œuvre*. This classical ideal is best represented in the **Oath of the Horatii** (see Plate I), emphasizing the necessity for sacrifice of life in the service of the State.

An extremist politically, he voted with *Robespierre* for the execution of *Louis XVI*. His brutally motivated **Marie-Antoinette on her way to the Guillotine** sketch, demonstrates clearly his anti-monarchist views. In contrast, **Marat assassinated** elevates an almost ludicrous murder (he was stabbed by Charlotte Corday while in his bath) to that of a Roman senator dying at his Emperor's command. It is here that David once again demonstrates his knowledge of Roman history. The Emperor Caligula initially insisted that all citizens should name him as principal heir in their wills. In times of financial difficulty, he would then "invite" them to honour their debts by committing suicide. Faced with an agonizing death if they failed to oblige, they often killed themselves painlessly.

David's revolutionary fervour was diluted by his time in the *Luxembourg*, after Robespierre's fall. In 1799 he met *Napoleon* and transferred his allegiances to *Bonapartism*. Despite the strong propaganda element, **Napoleon in his**

Words italicized (on their first appearance) in the text are explained in the Glossary.

Musée du Louvre

(Above) **DAVID Marie-Antoinette on her way to the Guillotine**
David's anti-monarchism is blatant here. In his hatred, he has robbed Marie-Antoinette of all queenly attributes. She sits with her arms cruelly pinioned, a plain, middle-aged woman. David voted for the death sentence for the King, and was exiled after the Bourbon restoration

(Below) **DAVID Marat assassinated**
David here combines personal resentment at the murder of his friend with a classical parallel. He likens Marat's murder to the death of a Roman senator who, at his Emperor's command, opens a vein in a hot bath. This is a dramatic depiction of the assassination of the artist's idol

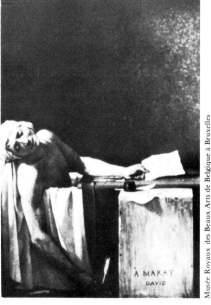

Musée Royaux des Beaux Arts de Belgique à Bruxelles

(Above) **DAVID Napoleon in his study**
The propaganda element in his picture is plain. The candles have burnt low, the clock shows a quarter past four; it is the early hours of the morning, but Napoleon is still at work for France

(Below) **DAVID**
Bonaparte crossing the St. Bernard
David's austere approach to art is admirably demonstrated in this picture, which elevates Bonaparte to the rank of a demi-god. The discipline of neo-classical art, founded on the portrayal of revolutionary idealism, is in marked contrast to the frivolities of the previous age, the laxity and immorality of which had disgusted him. On the rocks in the foreground are inscribed the names: Bonaparte, Annibal Karolus Magnus IMP

study is a magnificent example of David's incomparable skill as a portraitist. Young people flocked to his *atelier*. As the finest teacher of his day, it is interesting to find *Ingres*, *Gros* and *Girodet* numbered among his pupils.

David set himself up as the arbiter of technical standards. Using small brushes, he insisted on the total elimination of all visible strokes, imparting a glossy and finished appearance to his pictures. When in 1812 David visited the *Salon*, he paused before **The Cavalry Officer** by the young *Géricault*, examined it intently and declared, that he could make "nothing of this brush-work". It is interesting to note here the very basis of the future contretemps between *romanticism* and *classicism*.

This move away from intricate realism was the beginning of a new ideal, an escapist approach to the world of harsh reality. Extreme emotions occupied the thoughts of writers, poets and painters; the dramatic extremities of human attitudes, actions and passions, were enhanced by situations and settings matching the mood of the actors. The constant factor, which seems to have been completely overlooked by all participants, is the theatrical attitude struck by romanticist and classicist alike.

(Above) **DAVID The Coronation of Napoleon**
In this grand scale painting David, the official court artist, originally intended to portray Napoleon crowning himself, having unexpectedly seized the crown from the Pope's hands. Advised by Gérard to modify this, David shows Napoleon placing the crown on the head of Joséphine. David, at the Emperor's request, also included Napoleon's mother, although she was not present at the ceremony, and the Pope in the act of benediction

In his large scale pictures, **The Pesthouse at Jaffa** and **Napoleon at the Battle of Eylau**, Gros had anticipated the new trend. The magnitude of these pictures later served as inspiration to Géricault and *Delacroix*.

The *Ossian* poems by James Macpherson, however, proved one of the main inspirations for romanticism. The mythical adventures of this Celtic hero, called Fingal in Scotland, had been adopted by Napoleon. Girodet, a talented pupil of David, had undertaken at the Emperor's command a series of decorations for *Malmaison*. Although these were not completed, the preparation sketch brilliantly demonstrates the Bonapartist propaganda, allied to an informality of brush-work, which was later to be the very breath of romanticism.

In 1819 Géricault produced his masterpiece. The prison-ship "Medusa" foundered at sea off the coast of Senegal and Géricault composed an enormous canvas of the event (see Plate III). Visiting the local mortuary, he used corpses to evolve a ghastly pallor for the leaden colour scheme. He subjected all the elements in the picture to this vision; the sky and sea became embodied with human qualities of menace. He announced that the raft was

(*Above*) **GIRODET Ossian receiving the shades of French soldiers**
Based on James Macpherson's Ossian poems and their hero, the legendary Celtic bard hailed as the Homer of the North, this painting became a favourite of Napoleon. It was commissioned as the design for a ceiling in Malmaison and Girodet shows the French dead, encircled by sprites and flower-maidens, received into Valhalla

(*Below*) **GÉRICAULT**
Four studies of a severed head of a man
Géricault's fascination with death, like that of his young friend Delacroix, drove him to work from such grisly specimens. Pictures "redolent with romantic horror" were made the more arresting by the accuracy with which he depicted the ghastly pallor of death

(*Above*) **GROS Napoleon at the Battle of Eylau**
Gros' finest pictures are his battle-scenes, full of movement, colour, strength and vigour, of which this enormous canvas is an excellent example. Not exiled under the Bourbons like David, he astutely changed his decoration for the dome of the Panthéon from the apotheosis of Napoleon to that of the Bourbon restoration. He was made a baron by Charles X

(Above) **BOUCHER Louise O'Murphy**
Boucher, a superb technical craftsman, effectively decorated the Bourbon court with vast expanses of naked
flesh and mythological subjects. This charming study of
one of Louis XV's mistresses demonstrates both his
virtuosity and the atmosphere of Versailles

(Below) **FRAGONARD The Swing**
This light-hearted picture is typical of both the rococo
style and the decadence of the royal court. The lover who
sprawls before his mistress is said to have asked Fragonard
to portray a bishop pushing the swing. This was the
frivolous existence swept aside by the Revolution

(Above)   **CLAUDE**
          Landscape with Ascanius shooting the stag of Sylvia
Painted in the seventeenth century, this pays homage to traditional
narrative subject-matter. The inspiration is classical – a story from
the "Aeneid" – but Claude reduces the story to the smallest possible
proportion. He is principally interested in the landscape, but convention demands that the title should belie this

(Below) **POUSSIN Bacchanalian revel before a term of Pan**
Poussin, the greatest French painter of the baroque age, here depicts
the Titianesque, mythological scene. Later, lesser artists interpreted
this approach to the nude as the only acceptable vehicle for its
depiction

Hamburg Kunsthalle

(Above) **FRIEDRICH The Wreck of the Hope**
The innate forces of nature are awe-inspiringly depicted here. The "Hope", trapped in the Arctic ice, is destroyed by the long-awaited thaw which, instead of freeing the ship from the winter's clutch, crushes her with demoniac ferocity

Neue Nationalgalerie, Berlin

(Below) **INGRES Romulus vanquishing Acron**
Using a fragment of a Roman bas-relief after Phidias for the pose of Romulus, this picture, painted in 1812, typifies Ingres' approach to historical painting. The neo-classical ideal is found in the combination of the carefully chosen subject-matter and his matchless skill as a draughtsman

Paris, Ecole des Beaux-Arts

Musée du Louvre

(Above) **GROS Bonaparte at Arcole**
The young Bonaparte in Italy is painted here by his exact contemporary and ardent admirer in an idealized way. Gros, David's closest friend and follower, was introduced by Joséphine into the Napoleonic entourage

(Left) **FRIEDRICH**
Man and woman gazing at the moon
Friedrich, a German artist, is included here because his work breathes the fundamentals of romanticism. He injects into his pictures the intangible romantic essence. His landscapes assume human properties of mystery and menace; the claw-like roots and branches are emotional rather than naturalistic features

(Below) **CHASSÉRIAU The Toilet of Esther**
Delacroix soon emerged as the accepted leader of the school of romantic painters. This picture of 1841 clearly owes much to Delacroix and was described by Théophile Gautier as "of Greek taste and oriental savagery"

Musée du Louvre

(Above) **GÉRICAULT The Wounded Cuirassier**
This interesting study, painted after the fall of the
Empire, contrasts greatly with the martial appearance of
The Mounted Officer of the Guard, which was painted
before the ill-fated Russian campaign. In that picture,
the officer is dashing towards battle and glory, confident
of victory. Here, the cuirassier laboriously descends a
slope. He leaves the fray and, set against a romantic
background of smoke and fire, personifies his wounded
country

(Below) **GÉRICAULT**
The Race of the Riderless Horses
Following a visit to Rome in 1816, Géricault wished to
capture both the nude studies of Michelangelo and his
own passionate love of horses. This picture of the annual
race of riderless Barbary horses let loose in the Corso
seems to be classical in inspiration. Géricault's vivid light
and romantic impetuosity, however, inject a very
different atmosphere into the picture

France, drifting helplessly on the post-*Waterloo* political
seas, moved by any current or eddy. The young Delacroix
is said to have posed for one of the figures on the raft.

Géricault's influence was soon to be over, though. In
1824 he was injured in a riding accident and died shortly
afterwards. Delacroix was from then on destined to
dominate the scene of romantic painting. Rumoured to
be the illegitimate son of the diplomat *Talleyrand*, the
artist was soon recognized as the leading force among the
younger men. His controversial **Dante and Virgil in the
Inferno** behind him, Delacroix aroused fresh criticism
with his deeply moving **The Massacre at Chios** (see
Plate V) in 1824. "Dashed off in a small damp studio near
the Sorbonne", the **Massacre** embodied new vibrant uses
of brush-work, allied to a daring suggestion of space in the
background. Delacroix owed this to *Constable's* **The Hay
Wain** which was on show in Paris at this time. Although
the legendary repainting of the background in three days,
while it was actually on show in the Salon, is fictitious,
Delacroix was moved to repaint a large area of land and
sky, to accord with Constable's inspiration.

(Above) **CONSTABLE The Hay Wain**
Acting on Turner's advice, Constable submitted **The Hay Wain** to
the 1824 Salon where it was awarded the gold medal of merit. After
seeing the picture, Delacroix is supposed to have entirely repainted
the background of **The Massacre at Chios** in three days, while it
was actually on show in the Louvre. In fact, he saw **The Hay Wain**
in a Parisian dealer's and repainted the background of **The Massacre**
before he submitted it to the jury

14

Following the revolution in 1830, Delacroix personified the new emotions in his canvas **Liberty leading the People**. But the most significant event of Delacroix's life was to occur shortly after this. In 1832 the Count de Mornay was appointed ambassador to the Court of the Sultan of Morocco. A mutual acquaintance, the Count's mistress, the actress Mademoiselle Mars, persuaded Mornay to take Delacroix with him. The six-month visit provided the artist with inspiration for the rest of his life. Africa supplied him with a new range of subject-matter; horses fighting, lion and tiger hunts and, above all, exotic and mysterious men and women, "clad in white, like Roman senators or maidens as the Panathenaic frieze of the Parthenon."

The oriental conception of women secluded from the world is mirrored in **Algerian women in their quarters**, and presaged the erotic depiction of the *"odalisque"* in romantic painting throughout the period.

Meanwhile, in official circles, Ingres was establishing himself as the arbiter of taste for his era. His reputation, as one of the greatest portraitists of all time, had been made by his Napoleonic and Rivière pictures. Continuing the classi-

(Above) **DELACROIX**
Algerian women in their quarters
In 1832 Delacroix accompanied the Count de Mornay to Algiers, to the court of the Sultan at Meknès. The mysteries of the east which were revealed to him during this six-month expedition provided him with subject-matter for the rest of his life. He persuaded a renegade to allow him to sketch the inmates of his harem. The idea of women confined at the mercy of their master presented a fresh image of womanhood to France, echoing romantic parallels in contemporary novels such as Dumas' "The Count of Monte Cristo"

(Below) **GÉRICAULT The Mad Woman**
During his preparation for **The Raft of the Medusa**, Géricault frequented hospitals and mortuaries painting the insane, the dying and the dead. In 1821, shortly before his fatal riding accident, Géricault contracted to illustrate a book on madness for his friend, Dr. Georget, head of the Salpêtrière. This picture is one of a series of ten which he painted of lunatics

(Above) **DELACROIX Liberty leading the People**
The 1830 revolution inspired this picture. The romantic's intense desire for personal freedom and individualism is personified by the figure with the tall hat and blunderbuss – supposed to be a self-portrait. He steps forward to join the wounded worker, and joins the vision of Liberty, the daughter of Revolution, standing over the dead soldier and the rebel who are finally united in death

(Above) **INGRES Madame Moitissier seated**
During his long career, Ingres painted many such portraits of notable men and women. Like Velasquez before him, Ingres possessed a deeply sensitive appreciation of character, and also had a prodigious work-rate

(Below) **INGRES Angelica saved by Ruggerio**
This picture illustrates a scene from Ariosto's "Orlando Furioso", but was originally designed to represent the myth of Perseus and Andromeda. A classical scholar and archaeologist of note, Ingres demonstrates here the acceptable representation of the female nude as a mythological subject

cal themes of his master David, his **Vow of Louis XIII** for Montauban Cathedral was triumphantly received. So, except for a self-imposed exile between 1834 and 1841 when enraged by adverse criticism of his **Martyrdom of St. Symphorian** he applied for a teaching post as director of the French School in Rome, he dominated academic circles in Paris.

Although posterity has tended to condemn Ingres for his stubborn and sometimes vindictive opposition to Delacroix and the younger artists, his standards remained absolute. Dedicated to admiration of *Raphael* and emphasizing the integrity of drawing, Ingres' numerous imitators failed to maintain his vision. Official painting became stereotyped and repetitive.

Ingres continued all his life to paint in the grand manner, demonstrating his superlative technique in portraiture, mural-painting, nudes, and decorative and figure compositions. Attempting to show the dissenters his idea of the correct approach to art, Ingres set out to explore the

(Above left) **INGRES Napoleon on the Imperial Throne**
Painted in 1806, when he was twenty-six years old, this picture established Ingres as the greatest portraitist of the nineteenth century

(Above right) **INGRES The Dream of Ossian**
Many unlikely artists were attracted by the romantic Ossian theme. In England, John Sell Cotman painted a subject from Ossian; in France, Jean-Baptiste Isabey designed a frontispiece for the poems of Ossian; and even the young Ingres was influenced thereby. Here the traditional hero is seen celebrating the reconciliation of arms and poetry symbolized by the lyre

(Below) **DAUMIER Gargantua**
Based on a theme by Rabelais, Daumier depicts Louis-Philippe as a William-pear-headed giant. He gorges produce and, seated on a commode, excretes medals and certificates. This anti-monarchist cartoon earned Daumier six months imprisonment in Sainte-Pélagie

(Above) **INGRES La Source**
Ingres worked extensively from models throughout his life and this is a splendid example of the academic nude. It was against this ideal, which later became stereotyped, that Courbet, Manet, Renoir and Degas reacted

(Below) **INGRES The Turkish Bath**
This picture demonstrates Ingres' latent romanticism. Inspired by similar themes to those of Delacroix, the motivations are romantic and the interpretation classical. His sensual approach to the painting of the female nude, however, contrasts markedly with the almost mechanical precision of his portraits

potentialities of romanticism. His series of voluptuous nudes, among which are **La Source** and **The Turkish Bath**, merely underline the artificiality of his inspiration, and yet the excellence of his virtuosity.

At the same time another point of view was developing. Unselfconsciously, the caricaturist *Daumier* was commenting on the life he saw around him. Stripping his statements of artifice, he merely recorded what he observed in contemporary life. Usually he depicted in his cartoons the frailties of human nature; his droll sense of humour gibing at deputies, judges, lawyers, doctors and priests. Sometimes, however, his sense of justice was outraged and then he lashed out, as in **Rue Transnonain, 4 a.m.** and **Gargantua**. The latter representation of *Louis-Philippe* as a William pear seated on a commode, swallowing produce and excreting hollow paper qualifications and medals, earned him six months in the Sainte-Pélagie Prison!

In his spare time, despite his intense poverty, Daumier painted. His work was known only to a few intimates, *Decamps*, Rüet, *Millet*, *Théodore Rousseau*, *Corot* and Delacroix, who all admired him intensely. Although that

(Above) **DELACROIX The Jewish Wedding**
Delacroix attended a Jewish wedding in Tangiers in
February 1832, but did not paint this version of the
scene until 1841. It is the product of albums and sketch-
books the artist prepared there

(Below) **DAUMIER Don Quixote and Sancho Panza**
Although it would have been dismissed as unfinished by
his contemporaries, this brilliant canvas features all that
is best in Daumier's art. Shimmering with light, the
volume and expressiveness of the figures are superb

favourite term of the art critic, "unfinished", would have
been levelled against his painting, quite the antithesis of
his meticulous *lithographic* technique, Daumier nevertheless explored new dimensions in space, light and volume
in his work.

His range of subject-matter is extensive. He observed
candidly the washerwomen, the travellers, the harassed
mother, street musician, mountebank and the human
debris of Paris; all were subjected to his vision. Juxtaposed
passages of light and dark give emphasis and meaning to
vaguely sensed shapes. The gentle, short-sighted *Don
Quixote* theme appealed to him, and he repeatedly explored
its possibilities. In many ways Daumier's realism is genuine
social comment; comment, usually without innuendo,
merely recording in humanitarian terms the world and
people around him. A staunch republican, he rejected a
pension and the *Legion of Honour* in old age, and would
have died blind and penniless but for the generosity of
Corot. The latter purchased the house in Valmondois, in
which Daumier lived as a lodger, and in 1872 gave it to
him as a present.

This generous act was typical of the simple, quiet and
sensitive Corot. To him should really be accorded, in

(Above) **DAUMIER Don Quixote and the Windmills**
Daumier was fascinated by the Don Quixote story and based over
thirty paintings on the theme. He identified with both the rotund
Sancho and the near-blind aristocratic dreamer who tilted against
the windmills of society. This picture is remarkable for the design of
the masses, the chiaroscuro and, above all, the astonishing modernity
of the work

(Below) **COROT Avignon from Villeneuve**
This landscape, painted in 1835, Corot kept all his life. He rose at
4 a.m. every morning and scaled the hill at Villeneuve to paint
Avignon in the early morning sunshine. Corot, who painted often out
of doors, was one of the first artists to appreciate the importance of
the transience of light

(Above) **DAUMIER The Drama**
There are no political undertones here. Daumier merely
records what he sees around him of the life in Paris

his informal sketches, credit for the most significant
forward movement in nineteenth-century French landscape painting. Trained as a classical landscapist, and
heavily influenced by his Italian visits, Corot perfected in
the period 1830 to 1840 a fresh approach to landscape
painting. Above all, he realized the importance of the
transience of light to the artist. By painting on the actual
site, at the same time of day, over a number of days, he
anticipated in many ways the ideas later approved by the
Impressionists.

Corot had two approaches to painting. His official
style, embracing portraits, nudes and landscapes, which
he used for his Salon submissions, was very popular. This
was soft, shimmering, almost lyrical in quality, but was
composed from sketches, and suffered in the transformation to canvas. His less formal style showed a directness
of observation in his sketches which is without secondary
motivation; it contains none of the social attitudes then
prevalent in France, but merely demonstrates his love of
nature, and the spontaneity of his vision.

It is appropriate at this stage, before attempting to look
at the enormous contribution made by *Courbet*, to deal
with the other artists sharing, in some ways, Corot's
approach to painting.

The young English artist, *Richard Parkes · Bonington,*
had, in his Picardy landscapes, demonstrated something of

(Below) **DAUMIER The Card Players**
Although caricature intrudes to some extent in this
picture, Daumier's vision and perceptiveness make this
a remarkable genre-painting

(Above) **BONINGTON Near Boulogne**
The youthful Bonington, an Englishman working in France, conjured up visions of space in his pictures hitherto unparalleled on the Continent. Often working to proportions of three-quarters sky, one-quarter land, he created the impression of boundless space. Although he died at the early age of twenty-six, the feverish enthusiasm of the artist had already explored many influences and themes

(Below) **DELACROIX The Battle of Taillebourg**
This vast canvas was commissioned by King Louis-Philippe for Versailles in 1834. Based on Rubens' **The Combat of the Amazons**, the picture was cut down after completion, thus omitting the bridge. It depicts an episode from the war between Saint Louis and Henry III of England

the Constable approach to nature. This approach had been adopted by Delacroix, following Bonington's premature death in 1828.

At *Barbizon*, in the *Fontainebleau Forest*, a group of painters together derived their inspiration from nature. One of the group, Théodore Rousseau, although initially a romantic painter, went on to paint dramatic interpretations of nature's moods. He settled at Barbizon and there formulated a new style, based on the 17th-century Dutch landscape tradition of *Ruisdael*. It was a style with, what now appears to be, an almost "romantic additive". He was joined at Barbizon by *Diaz de la Peña*, and collectively they established a natural and precise method of recording peasant life and rural scenes, exactly as they saw them. They were occasionally visited at Barbizon by other artists: Corot, Courbet and *Daubigny* each stayed there at various times.

The most famous resident, however, was Jean François Millet. Inspired by Daumier, Millet rejected his earlier conceptions and, abandoning pastorals and almost-erotic nudes, turned to socialist themes. Dedicated to the ideal of the peasant labouring in communication with nature, and the nobility of poverty, Millet followed almost *Wordsworthian* traditions. He moved to Barbizon in 1849, and worked there for the rest of his life. With Rousseau and

(Above) **COROT Étang de Ville d'Auray**
In his later landscapes Corot achieves a compromise between a personal approach and the classical traditions he had acquired during his Italian visits. The light is diffused in silvery tones and a vaporous atmosphere is created

By courtesy of the Victoria and Albert Museum

(Above) **MILLET The Wood Sawyers**
Here Millet is pursuing his theme of the dignity of man engaged in a humble task, in communication with nature. He settled at Barbizon in the Fontainebleau Forest in 1849, but, unlike his companions there, he was interested in the people rather than the landscape. The dramatic picture has romantic undertones

(Below) **DAUMIER Counsel for the Defence**
Daumier, a staunch republican, had three great hatreds – for priests, doctors and lawyers. He hated the clergy most because they not only made profit, he said, from your birth, life and death, they also claimed your soul in the hereafter. Doctors and lawyers he hated for the same sort of reasons; the latter, he said, also robbed your children of their rightful inheritance after your death. This picture demonstrates only too clearly his opinion of the sentimental, acted oratory of counsel

Öffentliche Kunstsammlung, Basel

(Above) **COROT Italian girl at the fountain**
Corot, a highly skilled portraitist, also painted the female nude. In this painting, Corot owes much to Leonardo da Vinci's treatment of a figure. The Italian girl stands, bathed in contrasted light, before an idyllic pastoral scene which he handles with his customary charm

(Below) **DELACROIX Wall of Meknès**
A specimen page from the journal Delacroix kept throughout the expedition

Musée du Louvre

(Above) **MILLET Le Printemps**
A late canvas, this was to be one of four representing the seasons. His palette had by now been considerably enriched from his sombre beginnings, and the accuracy with which he records the light shows the extent of his understanding of nature. The artists, sporting their famous *barbes de bison*, went daily into the forest to paint

(Below) **DELACROIX The Death of Sardanapalus**
Based on an original inspiration from Byron, this picture represents the ultimate in human depravity. From his death-bed, Sardanapalus, a legendary king of Assyria, commands that his women and horses should be killed before his eyes, so that he can be certain that after his own death no one else will enjoy them. The grandeur, horror and extravagant setting are typical examples of romantic inspiration

Diaz, he shared the ambition to record exact and un-romanticized views of nature, but his earthy colours and peasant realism excited in his lifetime considerable controversy. Like his friend Daumier, Millet was too self-effacing to challenge forcefully both official and romantic attitudes. It was left to Courbet to mount a head-on confrontation with all these ideals, on behalf of so-called "nature and realism".

Arriving in Paris in 1840, the aggressive and singularly individual young man Gustave Courbet initially attended the *Académie Suisse*, which had been patronized, twenty years earlier, by Delacroix. Largely self-taught by frequent visits to the Louvre, Courbet determined to challenge the artificialities of existing traditions. He was influenced by the socialist ideals of *Prud'hon* and, despite his friendship with the intellectual *Baudelaire*, between 1843 and 1850 he painted three large canvases which were strongly anti-intellectual. He rejected all idealism and insisted on the democracy of realism. **The Burial at Ornans** was to

(Above) **MILLET The Angelus**
Millet once said: "A peasant I was born, a peasant I shall die." To him, people labouring in the fields were eternal biblical characters. Although this picture is regarded by some critics as a sentimental lapse, it shows the sincerity of Millet's rapport with simple people

(Above) **COURBET The Burial at Ornans**
Courbet, opposed to both neo-classicism and romanticism, strives here to portray the most real thing in life – death. This is not the death of a hero, it is the simple, commonplace death of a peasant, yet the figures are monumental, painted in sombre, funereal colours. This immense canvas was dismissed for "commonness and uselessness of thought, which are abominable", which criticism misses the rock-like reality of the scene

(Above) **DELACROIX**
Heliodorus driven from the temple
In 1858 Delacroix turned his energies to mural-painting. Working in the Church of Saint-Sulpice, near his studio in Place de Furstenberg, Delacroix reinterpreted Raphael's Stanze decorations

underline these theories, and indeed, at this time, it was nicknamed "The funeral of romanticism".

Courbet's **The Artist in his Studio** (see Plate VI) further aspired to be a manifesto of the role of the artist in society. When it was rejected by the Salon in 1855, Courbet took significant action; he hired primitive premises and exhibited it, privately, in what he called his "Pavilion of Realism". Although this merely attracted hostile criticism from the Press, it established the precedent of privately organized exhibitions.

Rabidly anti-clerical, Courbet's depiction of drunken priests in **Return from the Conference** aroused such hostility that a devout Catholic purchased the picture in order to destroy it. Gradually Courbet acquired the reputation of a dangerous fire-brand, both as artist and politician. The flagrant eroticism of some of his paintings of the female nude, such as the lesbian embrace in **The Sleepers**, caused moral rather than objective criticism to be levelled at his work. His naturalism and the unerring instinct of the countryman enabled him delightfully to depict aspects of everyday life, mountain and forest scenes, animals, still-life and floral compositions.

When in 1856 he painted **Young girls on the banks of the Seine**, Courbet took yet another forward step.

(Below) **COURBET The Sleepers**
The obviously erotic undertones of this and other portrayals of the female nude made Courbet notorious. The public outcry which often greeted his work obscured the consummate skill with which he depicted his subjects, heavy with sensuality and fleshly grace

23

Musée du Louvre

(Above) **COURBET La Roche Percée, Étretat**
Courbet's contribution to impressionism is most obvious
in this painting. Discarding for once his political and
socialist attitudes, he allows his painter's eye to record
simply what it sees

(Below) **COURBET**
The hunted roebuck on the watch
This remarkable picture reveals Courbet as the true
countryman, not as a town-dweller who anticipated
being called a yokel by proclaiming loudly his peasant
origin, but as a man steeped in knowledge of nature. His
obvious love of animals and his understanding of them
are in marked contrast to his political posturings

Musée du Louvre

Painting the background *plein air*, he superimposed the
figures afterwards in the studio. The picture was adversely
criticized, though, on the grounds of the moral abandon-
ment shown in the attitude of the girls. This criticism was
inspired by a prejudice originating in another picture,
The Bathers, which had been attacked on moral grounds,
too, even *Nadar* exclaiming: "Now that M. Courbet has
shown us his backside, what the devil will he come up with
next?" This therefore prejudged the reception of the
Young girls and, in the furore, his innovations were
overlooked.

During the 1860s the summer exodus to the Channel
ports, for the annual holiday by the sea, affected both
public and artist alike. Courbet was destined to meet the
American dandy *James Whistler*, the local painter, *Boudin*,
the young *Claude Monet* and others, in the holiday towns. It
was here that, in my opinion, his genius found its true
expression. In **The Sea** and **A Normandy Beach**

Musée du Louvre

(Above) **COURBET Young girls on the banks of the Seine**
This picture, painted in 1856, anticipates Manet's **Le Déjeuner sur
l'herbe** by seven years. Courbet painted the background "plein air"
and superimposed the figures in the studio. The importance of this
innovation was overlooked at the time by critics and public alike.
They complained about the abandoned posture of the girls, their
faces thickened and puffy with sleep and their – perhaps imagined –
air of promiscuity

(Above) **BOUDIN The Beach at Tourgeville-les-Sablons**
Boudin found Monet selling caricatures on the promenade at Le Havre and invited him to join him sketching. Later Monet said that it was "as if a veil had been lifted from his eyes"

(Above) **COURBET A Normandy Beach**
In common with the middle classes, Courbet enjoyed his annual holiday by the sea. He journeyed to the Channel ports during the period 1865–69 and, at Trouville, he met Corot, Boudin, Daubigny, Diaz, Monet and also the young American, James Whistler. The pictures Courbet painted here, particularly **The Sea,** greatly influenced the young Monet and, through him, the rest of the Impressionists

Courbet's style is stripped of artifice, and in these delightful pictures he anticipated the vision of the succeeding generation; they show his true destiny as a major precursor of *impressionism.*

Fate was to play a cruel trick on him. His political ambitions were apparently fulfilled when, in 1871, he was made president of a committee for the Preservation of Art, under the short-lived *Commune.* With typical maljudgement, Courbet became involved not in the preservation of art but in the demolition of the Vendôme column, a symbol of the Imperial past. After the fall of the Commune and a period of imprisonment in Sainte-Pélagie, like Daumier forty years before, in 1873 Courbet was unjustly ordered to pay an enormous indemnity. Forewarned of this, he fled from France, and died in exile at La Tour-de-Peilz in Switzerland in 1877. Thus, he had no say in that "clarification of purpose" embodied in the First Impressionist Exhibition of 1874.

While Courbet had been attacking the citadels of official art, another dissenting voice had been raised from within. Nothing could have been further from *Édouard Manet's* aims, than to have been cast in a role similar to

(Below) **COURBET Bonjour, Monsieur Courbet**
The arrogance of Courbet's attitude here, his thrust-out beard and his obvious self-sufficiency, caused a scandal. Depicting his meeting with Bruyas in the Languedoc, the subtlety of concealing the landowner's and gamekeeper's shadows under the larger shadow cast by a tree, whilst doubling his own image by an individual shadow, caused widespread resentment

(Above) **GIORGIONE Le Concert Champêtre**
The theme for **Le Déjeuner sur l'herbe** is taken from this picture. The highly praised treatment of the nude in this painting, a much admired Louvre masterpiece, prompted Manet to paint a contemporary version, for which he chose what he considered a more suitable title

(Below) **DELACROIX The Abduction of Rebecca**
This picture is based on an incident from Sir Walter Scott's novel "Ivanhoe". Delacroix thus daringly expanded his range of subject-matter, selecting romantic themes from various sources

that of Courbet. He was himself essentially of the establishment, and regarded the Salon as the only venue for his work. He felt, however, that official attitudes to subject-matter, and above all to the representation of the female nude, should be challenged. When in 1863 he followed up Courbet's **Young girls on the banks of the Seine** with a similar idea, he had little inkling of the controversy to follow. Basing his theme on a much-admired Louvre treasure, *Giorgione's* **Le Concert Champêtre**, popularly known as "Nymphs and Shepherds", Manet closely studied

(Above) **COROT**
Dardagny, a path in the country in the morning
In this picture Corot is on his favourite ground; the sunshine slanting through the trees and bushes floods the path in light and shadow

(Below) **COURBET La Roche de Dix Heures**
Painted near his beloved Ornans, glimpses of similar countryside may be seen in **The Burial at Ornans** and **The young women of the village.** It represents a typical landscape of the region of Franche-Comté. Courbet said, "Have you no country? To paint a region one must know it. I know my region and I paint it."

26

(*Above*) **MANET Concert in the Tuileries**
Even Baudelaire, who is depicted in this picture, was somewhat
reticent with his praise of the canvas. Brushed in with amazing speed
and dexterity, there is a fine modernist accent to this painting

(*Above*) **DELACROIX**
Hamlet and Horatio in the Churchyard
The dramatic passages in Shakespeare fascinated Delacroix; he was a distinguished scholar with a great knowledge of history, poetry and literature. As a young man
he had painted a portrait of himself as Hamlet

an engraving by *Marcantonio Raimondi* after a lost Raphael
picture, **The judgement of Paris**. He carefully posed a
group of people, including his brother Eugène, in a similar
attitude to a section of **The judgement**, then superimposed
the figures in his studio on to a landscape background, which
had been painted previously, "plein air". Following
Giorgione's inspiration, he depicted a nude female sitting,
unconcernedly, with males clad in contemporary dress. In
the left foreground, in the Dutch style, he arranged a still-
life group, consisting of the girl's discarded clothing, and
the eatables of the picnic. Instead of a title indicating the
picture's inspiration, he called it **Le Déjeuner sur l'herbe**
(see Plate XI).

As nearly 3,000 pictures, including Manet's submission,
were rejected that year by the Salon jury selection committee, the Emperor *Napoleon III* ordered these rejects
to be shown, in a separate but parallel exhibition to
be known as the "Salon des Refusés". No sooner had
Manet's picture been seen, than a storm of hostile criticism
burst out. Indeed, it was rumoured that the Emperor was
to charge Manet with indecency. Manet silenced his
opponents by revealing the sources of his inspiration.

(*Below*) **RAIMONDI The judgement of Paris**
(detail)
Manet used Raimondi's print, engraved after a lost
Raphael, for the posing of the three figures in his **Le
Déjeuner sur l'herbe**

27

(Above) **MANET Luncheon in the studio**
Manet reflects the ideas of the Dutch genre-painters in
this canvas. The carefully contoured still-life group in
the front left foreground is evocative of Vermeer. The
table is beautifully conveyed; the peeled lemon and
oysters are brushed in with the greatest economy. The
daring prominence of the foreground figure shows clearly
Manet's matchless virtuosity

(Below) after **HOKUSAI Design based on the Wave**
When Japan resumed trade with the West in 1854, after
years of isolation, her woodcuts soon flooded Europe.
The engraver, Braquemond, discovered Hokusai in 1856
and popularized his work. In the Paris World Fair of
1867, a large oriental pavilion proved a great success

(Above) **TITIAN The Venus of Urbino**
This was the source of another of Manet's brilliant interpretations –
Olympia was based on it. In lieu of the negress serving-maid and the
black cat, two women rummage through a chest in the background,
while a dog sleeps peacefully at the foot of the bed

Immediately the criticism moved from moral to technical
and aesthetic grounds.

Feeling that he had been misunderstood Manet disas-
trously attempted to clarify the situation. The next year he
continued his theme of painting contemporary versions of
accepted masterpieces of the past, and planned a modern
interpretation of *Titian's* **The Venus of Urbino**. Using
the same model, a girl named Victorine Meurent, he
submitted **Olympia** (see Plate XIII) to the 1864 Salon.
It was accepted, but no sooner exhibited than a storm of
protest again rang out. Demonstrations occurred, fists
were raised, umbrellas were shaken, shouting and laughter,
before "the odalisque with the yellow stomach". Amédée
Cantaloube thundered, "Women who are about to become
mothers, and young girls, would do well to avoid this sight
if they are wise". To his chagrin Manet was famous,
but certainly not in the manner for which he had longed.

From then on, he seemed unable to escape controversy.
When, the next year, he diverged from the Spanish mode,
made fashionable when Napoleon III had married a

Spanish wife, Eugénie de Montijo, to a Japanese source of inspiration, even Courbet ranged alongside his conservative critics. **The Fifer** was Manet's third major painting of Victorine Meurent. This time, she was clad as a boy fifer of the Imperial Guard. Influenced by Utagawa Kuniaki, whose print **The Wrestler** can clearly be seen in the background of Manet's portrait of *Émile Zola*, he dispensed, in the Japanese fashion, with a background to his figure. Courbet echoed the sentiments of most critics when he condemned the painting as looking like a playing-card. But this time Manet was not without supporters. Zola vigorously defended the picture, praising its translucence and charm "to the point of seductiveness". Manet, somewhat reluctantly, became the acknowledged leader of the "avant-garde set" at the Café Guerbois, a meeting-place of younger artists in Paris.

It was at this time that *Fantin-Latour* painted his group portrait **The studio in the Batignolles**. Numbered among the younger artists represented in the group paying homage to the master, scathingly referred to by the Press as "Manet's gang", were the significant figures of Monet, *Renoir* and *Bazille*. In the autumn of 1868 Manet, a great

(Above) **MANET The Fifer**
Here Manet dispenses with the background and interprets the figure in the Japanese style. The picture was rejected by the Salon of 1866, but was vigorously defended by Zola in "L'Événement". The model was again Victorine Meurent, the girl who posed for **Le Déjeuner** and **Olympia.** Strangely allied alongside the conservative critics of this picture was Courbet, who accused Manet of making pictures that looked like playing-cards

(Left) **FANTIN-LATOUR**
The studio in the Batignolles
A frequenter of the Café Guerbois in the Grande-Rue des Batignolles, Manet gradually became the focal point of a group of younger admirers, nicknamed "Manet's gang" by the Press. Fantin-Latour amazingly anticipates the eventual fame of the group; Manet sits at the easel painting the critic Zacharie Astruc; behind, facing us, is Zola; on his left, wearing a hat, is Renoir; Monet is on the extreme right in the background and, in the foreground, is Bazille

(Above) **MANET The Balcony**
Throughout his life Manet constantly borrowed subjects
and compositions from the old masters. Inclining to the
contemporary pro-Spanish feeling in France, which
stemmed from Napoleon III's marriage to Eugénie de
Montijo, Manet produced this canvas. It depicts his
future sister-in-law, the beautiful Berthe Morisot, the
painter Antoine Guillemet and a musician, Jenny Clauss

(Below) **GOYA Y LUCIENTES**
      Majas on the balcony
Manet's source of inspiration for **The Balcony**, Goya
painted this picture some fifty years earlier. The romantic
majas sit bathed in light, their quarrelsome escorts lurk
mysteriously behind

painter of women, featured a beautiful young girl, *Berthe Morisot*, in **The Balcony** – his interpretation of *Goya's* painting, **Majas on the balcony**.

The stage had been set for change for some time, and even four years earlier all the actors had been present in Paris. The young people had been loosely linked by two institutions, the Académie Suisse and a studio run by *Marc-Gabriel Gleyre*, famous for its liberality. The central figure at the Académie Suisse was *Camille Pissarro*, a West-Indian of Portuguese-Jewish descent, who had been in France since 1855 and had based his approach to painting on that of Corot. At Gleyre's studio was Claude Monet from Le Havre, who was to be the dominant figure in the Group. Other students there were Frédéric Bazille from Montpellier, *Alfred Sisley* of Anglo-French

(Above) **MANET The Execution of Maximilian** (detail)
Unfortunately only a fragment can be reproduced here. Manet left
the canvas behind when he vacated a studio; in his absence the
concierge chopped up the stretcher for firewood, and the canvas was
ruined by damp. Manet salvaged several fragments. There is a
preliminary study on view in the Kunsthalle, Mannheim. The
incident depicted is the murder of Maximilian, the Emperor of
Mexico, by the revolutionaries. Its exhibition was prohibited, as too
topical, until 1867

parentage, and Auguste Renoir from Limoges. Berthe Morisot had been the pupil of Corot since 1861 and, when Émile Zola's friend, *Paul Cézanne*, arrived from Aix-en-Provence, the cast was complete. In 1864 Gleyre's studio closed and Claude Monet persuaded his fellow students to join him at Chailly-en-Bière, in the Fontainebleau Forest outside Paris, to paint from nature. Thus one of the art world's most significant movements was born.

It is necessary at this point to retrace the sequence of events slightly. Young Claude Monet had been in Paris since 1859; the previous year Eugène Boudin had made the acquaintance of this young man in Le Havre. Monet at this stage in his life was selling caricatures of holiday-makers on the promenade! Boudin recognized his latent talent and invited him to come out sketching with him. Monet later said, "A veil was torn from my eyes and in a flash I saw what painting meant".

In Le Havre Monet had already met Boudin and was later to meet Corot, Whistler, Courbet, Daubigny and *Jongkind*. The latter, with Boudin, must be considered one of the major precursors of impressionism and was a formative influence on Monet. Jongkind painted water-colours

(Above) **MORISOT In the dining-room**
Berthe Morisot had studied under Corot when young and also became a close friend of Manet, after meeting him at the Louvre. Her feminine sensitivity is matched by the strength of her draughtsmanship. Throughout her life she remained constant to the impressionist ideal, and exhibited in seven of the eight Group exhibitions

(Below) **GOYA Y LUCIENTES**
         The Execution of Insurgents
         (May 3rd 1808)
Goya rightly regarded this as his finest picture; it is a masterpiece, emotionally capturing the horrific event. Manet used this as inspiration for **The Execution of Maximilian**

(Above) **ROUSSEAU Route in the Forest of Fontainebleau**
The vast distorted sky, treated in a romantic fashion, dominates this composition. The painting is reminiscent of a Dutch landscape, but the interpretation is typical of the colony of artists at Barbizon

31

(Above) **JONGKIND Street in Antwerp**
As early as 1863, Castagnary had used the word "impression" when criticizing a Jongkind painting. It is with the medium of water-colour that Jongkind achieves his best effects straight from the subject, using a fresh, dexterous approach

(Above) **DAUBIGNY View of the Oise**
Daubigny exhibited in the Salon of 1838, and is credited with being the first landscapist to work entirely out of doors. As a jury member of the Salon, he regularly voted for the younger artists, and is a major link between Barbizon and the Channel ports artists of the sixties. In 1857 he fitted out a studio houseboat and floated along the Oise painting riverscapes, recording hourly changes of light

(Below) **ROUSSEAU The Oaks**
The critic, Théophile Gautier, wrote of this picture, "Rousseau takes an oak and makes its portrait, as one would do that of a god, a hero or an emperor." It was painted out of doors, entirely from nature, and Rousseau himself remarked of it, "I hear the voices of the trees . . . They have suddenly revealed to me the language of the forest."

directly from nature out of doors and, before alcoholism and debauchery overwhelmed him to the point of madness, painted lively sketches on the Normandy sea coast and the Seine estuary.

François Daubigny successfully linked the Barbizon group of painters, before Monet's expedition there in 1864, with the young people who were later to be classed as the Impressionists. He has been credited as the first landscapist to paint entirely out of doors. For many years Daubigny was a jury member of the Salon selection committee and regularly, without much success, voted for the work of younger artists. He was a friend of Corot and since 1857 had specialized in what he called "riverscapes". He fitted out a houseboat, which he called "Le Botin", as a floating studio and drifted up and down the Oise, painting. Daubigny like Corot had already discovered the importance to the artist of the hourly changes in light. Indeed, when working at Trouville in 1865, he had been singled out as the leader of the "School of Impressions", while *Théophile Gautier* dismissed his work as "working sketches not paintings".

(Left) **I DAVID Oath of the Horatii**

Oil on canvas 130″ × 160″

This picture expresses the neo-classical ideal with its new moral fervour. Inspired by Corneille's "Horace", it represents the Roman virtue and glory of dying for one's country. In the centre is Horatius whose sons swear to fight the Curiatii to the death. Behind them the women are weeping for, whoever wins, they will be bereft of a husband, brother or lover. This painting, with its strong propaganda element, proudly depicts the conflict of personal feeling and public duty. The classical formality of the composition is typical of David

(Below) **II INGRES La Grande Odalisque**

Oil on canvas $32\frac{5}{8}″ × 42\frac{7}{8}″$

Ingres' art here was described by Lionello Venturi as "a frozen romanticism". The painter, although dedicated to the neo-classical ideal, was not a slave to the "antique". He was an excellent portraitist, and attempted romantic subjects in accordance with the popular trends. However, the brilliance of his technique dominates his finished canvases. His nudes are disciplined studies but painted with great sensuality. The model's theatrical accessories merely underline the artificiality of the title and the alleged inspiration

(Above) **III GÉRICAULT The Raft of the Medusa**
Oil on canvas $193\frac{1}{4}' \times 281\frac{1}{2}''$
This gigantic picture, in the spirit of romanticism,
expresses far more than the horror of the shipwreck.
Géricault compared the raft to post-Waterloo France.
He painted from the bodies in a mortuary to obtain the
ghastly pallor and, with corpse-like colours, he gave the
elements, too, human qualities of menace

(Right) **IV DAUMIER The Third-class Carriage**
Oil on canvas $26\frac{3}{8}'' \times 36\frac{5}{8}''$
Daumier, an anti-bourgeois republican, extolled the
working class. The passengers accept the discomforts of
the journey in silence, with resignation and an innate
dignity

(Opposite right) **V DELACROIX
The Massacre at Chios**
Oil on canvas $166'' \times 138\frac{1}{2}''$
This painting of the Turkish massacre of Greek Christians
in 1821, was adversely received by the Salon. The
resignation of the victims and the drama of the Turkish
horseman heighten the horror of the child attempting to
suckle at his dead mother's breast

34

Musée du Louvre

(Above)   **VI COURBET The Artist in his Studio**
Oil on canvas 141¼″ × 234¾″

Courbet subtitled this painting: "Realist allegory. In-
terior of my studio, fixing a phase of seven years in my
life as an artist." Allegorical figures–Poverty, Death,
Torture, the Prostitute, the Hunter, for example–have
been identified; a Priest and a Rabbi are clearly discern-
able. On the extreme right, reading a book, sits Baudelaire, while Champfleury, a champion of Courbet's art,
is on the left of the couple next to him. Possibly they are
the allegories of suffering humanity and its oppressors.
But their united significance is through Courbet, who is
seated like a king in the centre of his court. He paints his
two great loves, a landscape of Ornans and his model, the
nude who stands watching. Of the little boy, Courbet is
said to have remarked that only he was pure enough to
understand his intentions

(Right)   **VII MILLET The Gleaners**
Oil on canvas 33⅛″ × 43¾″

Millet employed the colours of nature and faithfully
recorded the scenes around him. Unlike Daumier, he was
not politically motivated; his painting is simple comment
on the life of peasants he knew and loved

36

Musée du Louvre

Marcel Beurdeley Collection

(Left) VIII COROT The Belfry at Douai
Oil on canvas $18\frac{1}{4}'' \times 15\frac{1}{8}''$
This wonderful canvas, painted when Corot was 75, anticipated the impressionist depiction of light. An example of his "hazy" manner, it retains the spontaneity of a "plein air" sketch

(Below left) IX DELACROIX Marine View
Oil on canvas
Many of the innovations of the Impressionists were based on Delacroix's daring use of colour. This untypical "plein air" sketch dated from the Channel ports period, and clearly anticipates, both in paint texture and colour combinations, the Argenteuil era

(Below) X COROT The Church at Marissel
Oil on canvas $21\frac{5}{8}'' \times 16\frac{1}{2}''$
Besides the silvery-greys and greens of his popular idyllic pastoral scenes, Corot painted directly from nature. These scenes are regarded as his best works, and were based on the discoveries he made during his two-year stay in Italy. This lovely canvas is sensitively lighted and painted with consummate skill. An air of complete tranquillity pervades the whole

Musée du Louvre

(Right) **XI MANET Le Déjeuner sur l'herbe**

Oil on canvas $82\frac{3}{4}'' \times 106''$

Manet posed his favourite model, Victorine Meurent, nude, next to his clothed brother, Eugène and his brother-in-law, Ferdinand Leenhoff, in the studio. Posing them after a lost Raphael cartoon, he superimposed them on to a canvas of a woodland glade previously painted "plein air". The picture was rejected by the Salon and caused a scandal when exhibited in the "Refusés". It was considered an offence to public decency, because of the combination of a nude and clothed figures in an everyday setting. Manet was contesting the moralistic attitude to the depiction of the female nude as well as the conventions of titling and subject-matter; but this explanation did little to mitigate the enormity of his offence in the eyes of the critics

(Below) **XII BAZILLE The Family Reunion**

Oil on canvas $59\frac{5}{8}'' \times 91\frac{3}{8}''$

Bazille returned from Chailly to his native Languedoc to begin this painting. He posed his family on the Terrasse at Méric and recorded his idea of a grand scale picture in the open air. Features, such as the capturing of the play of light through the branches, owe much to the new cult of photography

Musée du Louvre

Musée du Louvre

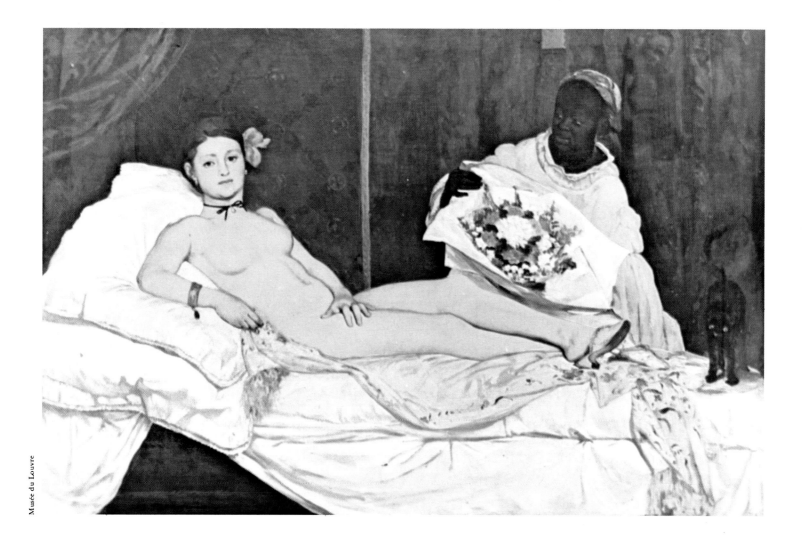

(Above) **XIII MANET Olympia**

Oil on canvas $51\frac{1}{4}'' \times 72\frac{3}{4}''$

Manet was inspired by Goya's **Maja Nuda** and Titian's **Venus of Urbino,** yet caused a scandal again when the picture was submitted to the 1865 Salon. He used the model, Victorine Meurent, for the nude figure, and gave the painting the title of a goddess–but the public refused to accept her as such. They imagined erotic significances, undreamt by Manet, in the negress, the black cat, and in Olympia's jewellery and black neck-ribbon

(Left) **XIV MONET La'Grenouillère**

Oil on canvas $29\frac{3}{8}'' \times 51\frac{3}{8}''$

Monet and Renoir often painted at this bathing and boating centre near Paris. Described by Maupassant in one of his short stories, "une grenouille" was a slang name not for a prostitute but for the easy amateurs of the locality. The most striking feature is the use of short, rapid strokes to give the rippling effect of the water. The technique is not wholly pointillist, since Monet confines it to this area only

39

Musée Marmottan, Paris

(Above) **XV MONET Impression Sunrise**

Oil on canvas $18\frac{7}{8}'' \times 24\frac{3}{4}''$

It was from this "plein air" painting that the name "impressionism" was coined. Exhibited in the first Exhibition of 1874, it was mockingly described as "the impression of a painting"–the critic wittily parodying the title. The name was apparently acceptable to artists and critics alike, and was used from then on

(Right) **XVI MONET Le Déjeuner sur l'herbe**

Oil on canvas $51\frac{1}{8}'' \times 73''$

This painting, dedicated to Manet's ideal, is one of the most important in French nineteenth-century art but, unfortunately, the original is lost to posterity. It was left unfinished when Monet turned to painting **Women in the Garden,** and was ruined by damp. Only two fragments of the original survive. This is a preliminary study identical in intention to the giant, grand scale picture Monet worked on for so long in the forest of Chailly

Pushkin Museum, Moscow

(*Above*) **XVII SISLEY The Saint-Martin Canal**
Oil on canvas $19\frac{5}{8}'' \times 25\frac{5}{8}''$
Sisley demonstrates in this landscape, exhibited in the
Salon of 1870, the technique discovered by Renoir and
Monet the previous year at "La Grenouillère". These
experiences continued to influence Sisley for the rest of
his life, and he remained the typical impressionist,
retaining the mode of the seventies until his death

Musée du Louvre

(Above) **XIX PISSARRO**
Entrance to the village of Voisins
Oil on canvas 18″ × 22″

This picture was painted during Pissarro's interlude at Pontoise, when he gathered around him a group of artists working parallel to Monet and Renoir at Argenteuil. Frequent visitors were Cézanne, Sisley and Guillaumin. This picture follows a theme frequently used by Corot: the perspective of a road losing itself in the distance. The skill with which he uses the shadows cast by the trees to explore the ground surface is masterly

(Opposite left) **XVIII RENOIR Nude in the Sun**
Oil on canvas $31\frac{1}{2}$″ × $25\frac{1}{8}$″

This picture, exhibited in the Second Impressionist Exhibition of 1876, is sometimes called "Torso d'Anna". Renoir's delightful idea of posing the nude out of doors, dappled by the diffused effect of sunshine through leaves, accords with his statement: "All I want is a skin which does not repel the light."

43

(Right) XX MORISOT Hide and Seek
Oil on canvas

Unlike the other impressionists, Berthe Morisot painted few landscapes. The influence on her of Manet and Degas is clearly demonstrated by her preference to depict people. In this spirited canvas, however, she shows her "singularité", setting her delightful study of a mother and child in a superb landscape.

John H. Whitney Collection, U.S.A.

(Below) XXI DEGAS The Rehearsal
Oil on canvas 23″ × 33″

Degas delighted in the disciplined movements taught in the classes for ballet. He rarely painted the finished performance, but preferred to catch the dancers at informal moments. Despite their apparent spontaneity, his pictures were not produced "in situ" but from memory, aided by rudimentary sketches. The daring use of the spiral staircase which occupies the left foreground, and the light streaming through the windows behind the dancers, are typical Degas innovations.

The Burrell Collection, Glasgow Art Gallery and Museum

(Above) **XXII DEGAS The Bath Tub**
Oil on canvas $23\frac{5}{8}''\times 32\frac{5}{8}''$

Degas had an almost clinical approach to painting the female nude There is none of the sensuality to be found in the work of Ingres or Renoir, nor the eroticism in that of Courbet. In the 1886 Exhibition, Degas showed ten pastel nudes which he described as "a series of nudes of women bathing, washing, drying, rubbing down, combing their hair, or having it combed". He felt that before "the nude has been represented in poses which presupposed an audience"; these, in contrast, were studies

(Left) **XXIII CÉZANNE Apples and Oranges**
Oil on canvas $30''\times 37\frac{1}{5}''$

This superb composition, produced between 1895 and 1900, is one of the finest Cézanne created from familiar objects. No other artist has ever made such exciting an interpretation of commonplace things. He exhaustively examined the structure and presence of each item, "setting one colour against another, causing complementaries to vibrate, greens against reds, yellows against blues, leaning one fruit forward, another to the side, balancing them to obtain the desired effect"

45

(*Above*) **XXIV SEURAT Bathing at Asnières**
Oil on canvas $79\frac{5}{8}''\times118\frac{1}{8}''$

This, the first of Seurat's large scale compositions, is reproduced here
not for its pointillist attainment but for its influence on the world of
impressionism. The speckled brushmarks, contrasts of tints and
formalization of the figures, obviously anticipate the more positive
pointillist achievements of **Sunday Afternoon at La Grande Jatte.**
Durand-Ruel took this picture to New York in 1886 with 300 impressionist canvases. It was well received and contributed greatly to
Durand-Ruel's conquest of the American market

(*Right*) **XXV TOULOUSE-LAUTREC
At the Moulin Rouge**
Oil on canvas $47\frac{1}{4}''\times55''$

Lautrec once remarked: "seat me at a table, place a
glass of cognac before me and I am the equal of any man
alive." This famous canvas shows him at a dance-hall in
Montmartre with his cousin Gabriel Tapié de Céleyran
and others. In the background "La Goulue" is arranging
her hair. The mask-like face of Mlle. Nelly, illuminated
by a green off-stage light, shows the influence on him of
Japanese prints and of his idol, Edgar Degas

46

(Left) **XXVI RENOIR**
Le Moulin de la Galette
Oil on canvas $30\frac{1}{2}'' \times 45''$

This painting, produced in the open air, was not completed until 1876. His friends carried the picture daily to the top of Montmartre, and Renoir painted three versions of this scene. He loved the lower-middle-class families there, and many of the people are portraits of his friends

(Below left) **XXVII GAUGUIN Two Tahitian Women**
Oil on canvas $37'' \times 28\frac{3}{4}''$

This picture was painted at a time of great personal suffering during his second stay in Tahiti, the year after his abortive suicide attempt. Despite this, the exotic loveliness of the two girls is brilliantly captured. Without artifice, they are indeed "Eves living in Paradise, chaste yet sensuous, dark bodies full of promises, large eyes full of mysteries"

(Below) **XXVIII GAUGUIN The Yellow Christ**
Oil on canvas $36\frac{3}{8}'' \times 28\frac{3}{4}''$

This, the most successful of Gauguin's synthetist pictures, was painted in 1889 during his trip to Brittany. Taking something of the colours of the south to the bleaker peninsula, he visited Tremalo near Pont-Aven. He used the carved wooden crucifix there and arranged three women in folk costume around the cross. He wrote: "Don't copy nature too much. Art is an abstraction. Derive this abstraction from nature while dreaming in front of it, but think more of creating than of the actual result."

(*Opposite above*) **XXIX VAN GOGH**
The Starry Night
Oil on canvas 29″ × 36¼″
No picture ever painted more brilliantly reflects the
inner tensions and turmoils of its creator. The sky is alive
with movement, tormented spirals contrast with the
obalisk-like cypress, soaring heavenwards in flame-like
writhings. The passionate power of the visionary, however, is balanced by the masterly precision of the construction

(*Opposite below*) **XXX VAN GOGH**
Cornfield with Crows
Oil on canvas 20″ × 40¾″
His last picture. Shortly after completing it he shot
himself in the stomach. The fitful sky, fleeting birds and
swirling corn reflect the brooding melancholy with which
his persisting depression burdened his soul

On reaching Fontainebleau Monet and his friends began
painting. There they made the acquaintance of Théodore
Rousseau, Diaz and Millet. They painted forest interiors
directly from nature and Monet in particular was much
influenced by Diaz. During the winter of 1865 Monet
shared Bazille's studio in the house previously occupied by
Delacroix in the Rue de Furstenberg, and returned to
Chailly in the spring.

An interesting painting of this time is Renoir's **Inn of
Mother Anthony**; simply painted, it shows Renoir and
Sisley in Mère Anthony's tavern. The background walls
are covered with daubs and graffiti, made by the convivial
group of friends seeing for the first time the famous *barbes
de bison* affected by the older generation of artists, and
rhymed in a popular song of the day with Barbizon. It
was the sort of comradeship which so vitally affected the
artists at this time. Monet began immediately at the age
of twenty-five, what was to be his proclamation of open-air
painting as the very essence of revolutionary technique.
Conceived on a vast scale, Monet's **Le Déjeuner sur
l'herbe** (see Plate XVI) was to be larger and more direct
than Manet's. He was determined to paint the entire
picture out of doors, and persuaded Camille Doncieux, his
future wife, Bazille and others to act as models for him in
the natural attitudes of picnickers on the grass.

Courbet, on hearing of Monet's project, came out to

(*Above*) **MONET The Bridge at Argenteuil**
The work produced at Argenteuil strengthened the
proposition, made before the war, to hold an independent
exhibition. Encouraged by Nadar, the photographer,
who loaned them his studio, this resolution crystallized
in the 1874 Group Exhibition. In this picture Monet
deploys a slight variation on the impressionist theme,
using shorter, thicker strokes applied in an impasto
manner

(*Below*) **DIAZ DE LA PEÑA The Storm**
This emotional rendering combines the full force of
romanticism with the direct, Barbizon approach to the
depiction of nature. Diaz's exact and unembellished
renderings had considerable influence in the early 1860s
on the young Monet and his friends

49

(Above) **RENOIR**
Path winding up through tall grass
This picture, painted during the 1873–74 Argenteuil period, is typical of Renoir's charm and ability as a landscapist. The hillside and path are drenched with light. He frequently went painting with Monet

(Below) **MONET Women in the Garden**
Le Déjeuner sur l'herbe was unfinished, so Monet submitted this work to the 1867 Salon in its stead. He painted it entirely "plein air" and posed his wife, Camille, in various dresses. He hung the canvas from a tree and dug a pit beneath – to work on the upper sections he lowered the canvas into the trench

Chailly to see this huge picture (it measured fifteen feet by twenty feet) for himself. Monet greatly appreciated Courbet's advice and interest and, above all at this time, his financial assistance. Monet was forced, however, to cease work on this large undertaking for several reasons. Firstly, he had intended to submit it to the 1866 Salon but, when he realized that he could not meet the date deadline, he abandoned work in order to give himself sufficient time to produce a smaller picture painted in accordance with his dream. Zola later said that this was the dream of every painter, "to put life-sized figures in a landscape". Thus he produced his study of Camille entitled **Women in the Garden**, painted entirely "plein air", and submitted that to the Salon instead. Secondly, the cost of providing paint for such a large area was proving exorbitant, and consequently he left patches unfinished. Thirdly, he had repainted several sections, acting on Courbet's advice, and then keenly regretted having done so.

He still had the canvas in his possession as late as January 1878, when he left it as surety with his landlord at Argenteuil against unpaid rent. When he retrieved the picture in 1884 he found that it had been partly spoiled by damp; he cut away the ruined sections, and thus it is that only the central fragment survives. The preliminary design is still in existence, however, and is now in the Pushkin Museum of Modern Western Art in Moscow. This picture (see Plate XVI), although only $51\frac{1}{8}'' \times 73''$,

(Above) **BOUDIN Beach at Trouville**
Boudin's contribution to impressionism was considerable. He painted on the Channel coast all his life, patiently recording the hourly changes of light

(Above) **DEGAS Spartan girls and boys exercising**
Early in his career, Degas often painted historical subjects, following the classical tradition. In this canvas he represents Lycurgus and the women of Sparta watching the adolescents at their games. Gradually, Degas turned for his inspiration to life around him, but he returned to historical subjects for a considerable time and, in this, differed completely from his colleagues

(Above) **DEGAS Two Laundresses**
This is a late Degas. He captures the fleeting moment splendidly, contrasting the yawning inertia of one laundress, with the muscular intensity of the other

conveys an excellent idea of the finished concept.

The next few years saw the development of the technique which was later to be known as impressionism. Manet's patronage of the Café Guerbois provided a focal point so necessary for the formative artists, writers and dilettantes, where the caustic personality of *Edgar Degas* began to play an important role. Degas was a former student of Louis Lamothe, a pupil of Ingres at the *École des Beaux-Arts*. By 1860 Degas had produced **Spartan girls and boys exercising**, an historical painting in the masters' tradition, and was gradually working towards the total rejection of the Salon as a venue for his art. With Manet he dominated the conversation at the Café, and by his revolutionary attitude, his ideas on the informality of composition, and Japanese influences, enabled Monet and his friends to crystallize their ideas. They were joined frequently by the two most famous art critics of their day, Émile Zola and Edmond Duranty. To some extent Monet and his friends repudiated Parisian life; as Monet wrote in a letter to Bazille in 1867, "We have been too much concerned with what we see and hear in Paris".

(Below) **HIROSHIGE Moonlight Nagakubo**
The dynamic silhouettes and incisive outlines bounding pure, flat tonal areas, appealed to France. Instead of merely copying the mode blindly, Manet, Degas and others sought to harmonize the Japanese simplifications with an occidental viewpoint

51

S.P.A.D.E.M. Paris 1974

(Above) **MONET Rouen Cathedral in sunlight**
During the 1890s, Monet carried his exploration of the transience of light one stage further. He began a series of pictures depicting the changing moods which the façade of Rouen Cathedral evoked by different light effects. He recorded the cathedral in grey weather, morning light, mist and full sunlight

(Right) **RENOIR La Grenouillère**
Throughout 1869, Renoir and Monet were constant companions on painting expeditions. La Grenouillère, on the Seine, is featured several times in their work of this period. It was a popular boating and bathing place, and is mentioned in the works of Maupassant and other contemporary writers

Renoir and Monet turned to the banks of the Seine for inspiration. The painters selected the "La Grenouillère" area, a spot later frequented by *Maupassant* and featured in several of his short stories. Monet and Renoir each painted several versions of the landing-stage on the island, the bathers, boats and, above all, the diffused gleams of sunlight dancing on the dappled surface of the river.

This was a period of great financial hardship for the young painters; indeed only the generosity of Bazille at times stood between Monet and actual starvation. Bazille had returned to his native Montpellier and was working on a similar theme to that of Monet, a grand scale painting in the open air. Assembling his family at Méric near Montpellier in Languedoc, he painted them on the terrace of the family estate there. Again like Monet and Renoir at "La Grenouillère", he concentrated on the depiction of the dappled effect of sunlight filtering through the trees. This idea culminated in 1876 with Renoir's magnificent tribute to light, **Le Moulin de la Galette** (see Plate XXVI).

Meanwhile Pissarro had emulated the others. He moved to Louveciennes and set up his easel there, and at Bougival. Working on the theme of Corot's **The Sèvres Road**, he set out to depict roads viewed in perspective, and disappearing

Nationalmuseum, Stockholm

(Above) **JONGKIND Moonlight**
Jongkind was a Dutchman working in France, who was closely associated with the artists painting at the Channel ports in the 1860s. Despite his penchant for alcohol and debauchery, his deftness of touch gained him a well-deserved reputation as a landscapist. He worked mainly on the Seine estuary and along the Normandy coast

(Above) **MONET Poppies**
In 1873 Monet, working with Renoir at Argenteuil, produced this picture at the same time that the latter painted his **Path winding up through tall grass.** The intention is similar – to depict a field sloping upwards, this time dotted with poppies painted in comma-like dots, shining through the pale green of the grass

ultimately in the haze of infinity. A number of fine pictures date from this time; **The diligence at Louveciennes** is one which achieves a magnificent effect of rain and muddy reflections at dusk in the autumn. Using both horizontal shadows, as in the **Entrance to the village of Voisins** (see Plate XIX), and light shafting between houses, as in **The Road at Louveciennes**, he brilliantly explored the structure of the ground surface.

Alfred Sisley was by now associating with the Group. His financial circumstances were comfortable, and he was able to work in a dilettante fashion. Jongkind's decision to live at Montmartre provided new surroundings and new subject-matter. The artists, including *Armand Guillaumin*, a close friend of Cézanne and Pissarro, frequently painted the windmills and narrow streets of the rambling village outside Paris.

On July 18th, 1870, the *Franco-Prussian war* broke out. Like any group of young people, the individual reaction was different in each case. Manet joined his unit of the National Guard, in which he already held the rank of lieutenant. Degas joined the artillery; Renoir enlisted in the

(Below) **MONET The Magpie**
In this picture, Monet covers similar ground to that of Pissarro in **Snow at Lower Norwood.** The light effect, occasioned by the subtle shadows on the snow, is the particular point of interest for Monet

(Above) **SISLEY Boat-races at Hampton Court**
If Sisley did flee to England in 1870, as did Monet and Pissarro, nothing is known about his visit. Some art historians now think that it is highly unlikely that he ever left France during this period. His work, however, was known in London by 1872. In 1874 he stayed at Hampton Court and Molesey, and this picture probably dates from this successful stay. It is remarkably spontaneous in technique and sparkles with light and life

(Below) **PISSARRO Snow at Lower Norwood**
With the outbreak of the Franco-Prussian war, Pissarro fled to England. He painted this delightful canvas when living in the London suburbs. His entire pre-1870 work was destroyed when the Germans looted his studio in Louveciennes, which he had abandoned before the Prussians invaded

(Above) **PISSARRO The Station at Penge**
Another product of Pissarro's 1870 stay in England, this was possibly influenced by the art of Turner, whom he described as using "tinted steam" in his pictures. This picture was essentially based on a modern theme and anticipates Monet's **La Gare Saint-Lazare, Paris** by several years

cavalry; Bazille volunteered for the Zouaves; and Monet fled to England, as did Pisarro, Daubigny, Sisley (perhaps) and *Durand-Ruel*, a sympathetic art dealer ultimately of great significance to the group. Cézanne, too, ignored the call to arms and retired to L'Estaque, near Marseilles, where he lived with an artists' model, Hortense Fiquet.

The war, which is now almost forgotten, tragically brought about the death of Frédéric Bazille. Serving in a "corps d'élite", he was killed in action at Beaune-la-Rolande, on November 28th, 1870. Thus fell the spiritual leader of the Group. With tragic irony his last recorded remarks, spoken the evening before his death, expressed the characteristic optimism with which he faced life: "As for me I am certain I shall not be killed; I have too many things to do in my life." Alas for posterity, he fell the next morning, a few days short of his twenty-ninth birthday.

The enforced visit by Monet and the others to England had some significant results. Apparently ignorant initially of each other's whereabouts, Pissarro sought refuge at Lower Norwood, and Monet was also in London; they met accidentally through Paul Durand-Ruel, who had opened a gallery at 168, Bond Street. Although where Sisley actually stayed is unknown, he also was probably in England, as was Daubigny who was busily engaged in painting, and selling, views of the Thames.

Almost penniless, Pissarro and Monet painted together. Years later Pissarro wrote: "Monet and I were thrilled with the landscapes in London . . . we painted directly from nature . . . I made studies of fog effects, of snow and springtime . . . Monet painted several superb studies of fog in London. We also visited the museums. The paintings and water-colours of *Turner* and Constable, as well as canvases by Old *Crome*, certainly influenced us . . ."

The war and the Commune over, during 1872 the members of the Group began to drift back to Paris. Manet first visited his family in the Pyrenees where they had taken refuge. Monet returned via Holland where he painted several notable canvases. His first act on reaching Paris was, accompanied by Boudin, to visit Courbet in the Sainte-Pélagie Prison. Durand-Ruel on his return moved his gallery to Rue Laffitte. Degas was also in Paris for a short while before setting sail for New Orleans. Renoir meanwhile spent a two-month holiday at a friend's

(Above) **DEGAS The Musicians of the Orchestra**
This splendid canvas depicts Désiré Dihau, the bassoon soloist at the Opera and mutual friend of Degas and Toulouse-Lautrec

(Below) **SISLEY Market-place at Marly**
Between 1872 and 1876 Sisley painted at Louveciennes and Marly. This delightful canvas demonstrates all that is best in his work. He once said that "the spectator should . . . follow the path indicated for him by the painter, and see what has caught the painter's eye"

(Above) **TURNER Rain Steam and Speed**
We know that Pissarro saw this picture during his stay in London for, several years later, he mentions it in a letter to his son, Lucien, as "the famous picture of the train". This painting is heavily mannerized by Turner's mature romantic vision of contorted clouds, steam, light, fog and water

(Above) **PISSARRO La Côte des Boeufs, Pontoise**
When Pissarro had first arrived in France, he had written to Corot asking if he might style himself "the pupil of Corot", rather than use his own name. The feathery spread of the tree branches shows how closely akin is his work to that of his mentor

(Below) **MORISOT Jour d'été**
Berthe Morisot's "summer's day" shimmers with light and movement. She, more than any other, influenced Manet to effect such a radical change in style, so late in life. Successfully combining the role of artist with that of wife and mother, her contribution to the evolution of impressionism is a most important one

château in the south. Pissarro, returning to Louveciennes, discovered that the invading Prussians had looted his studio during his absence and destroyed all the pictures stored there. Sick at heart, he moved to Pontoise.

It was now that Monet made a momentous decision. He settled in Argenteuil on the Seine, where, forsaking figure painting, he turned all his energies to landscape. He was quickly joined by Renoir, the now impoverished Sisley and indirectly by Manet. Indirectly, because Manet's brother Eugène had meanwhile, in 1874, married Berthe Morisot and they settled at Argenteuil. Manet frequently visited them there and a new era in art was about to begin.

Monet had stayed in Argenteuil on several occasions before the war, and from 1872 to 1878 made his home there. Situated just outside Paris, the village was a favourite spot for boating enthusiasts. Monet and Renoir re-established their famous painting duets. Many obvious examples could be quoted to demonstrate this fruitful companionship; probably the best comparison is between

(Above) **PISSARRO The Seine at Marly**
When he returned from England after the war, Pissarro moved from Louveciennes and settled at Pontoise, near the Oise. Sisley had moved to Marly, which is on the Seine not far from Argenteuil. Visiting him there, Pissarro painted this picture on the riverside. The continued contact between the constituent members of the Group, and their common intention, is obvious when this picture is compared with the contemporary works of Monet and Renoir

56

Lady Aberconway, Private Collection, London

Renoir's **The Seine at Argenteuil** and Monet's **Sailboats at Argenteuil**, painted simultaneously from identical vantage points.

Copying Daubigny, Monet set up a houseboat as a floating studio and worked from it. Manet painted two versions of him accompanied by his wife Camille, sketching on "Le Botin". The pictures produced there are the very soul of impressionism. The analysis of light, by breaking down the colours into component primaries and secondaries, produces a spectral mixture. They used many of the innovations of Delacroix and, by lowering the tone of a pigment by the introduction of its complementary colour, the artists discovered new dimensions in the representation of nature.

Manet then began to work in the new technique also. The lovely **Bank of the Seine at Argenteuil** shows to advantage his clear-cut vision and virtuosity. Combining his own excellence of line and rapid brush-work with the new ideals, the canvas shimmers with sunlight and movement. He produced several fine pictures during these years but never completely adopted the so-called impressionist technique without some personal reservations.

This period for Monet and the younger artists was one of critical financial difficulty. Even Durand-Ruel was forced to withdraw his support for a time. The Salon was implacably hostile and no other venue for sales existed.

(Left) **MANET Bank of the Seine at Argenteuil**
This picture demonstrates how completely Manet had been won over to the impressionist ideal. With his incomparable good taste, he readily achieves a compromise, fusing his love of the human figure with landscape and atmospheric light

(Above) **SISLEY Flood at Port Marly**
Painted during the floods of 1876, this picture contains many of the elements of light, shimmering and reflecting on water, similar to previous successful attempts by Monet and Renoir. It is a fine demonstration of Sisley's mastery of the impressionist technique

(Below) **MONET Sailboats at Argenteuil**
Using larger, bolder masses of colour, Monet explores yet another variation of the impressionist motif. The sail is drawn with a single stroke, and the tones are juxtaposed in rhythmic patterns

(Above) **MANET Monet painting on "Le Botin"**
Following Daubigny's inspiration, Monet fitted out a studio-boat named "Le Botin". Manet painted this picture of him at work with his wife Camille looking on, when he visited his brother Eugène and his sister-in-law Berthe Morisot who were staying at Argenteuil. Delighted by the new theories, Manet demonstrated his receptiveness by adopting the impressionist technique himself

(Below) **RENOIR The Box**
Renoir's brother, Edmond, posed for the man here, an unknown model for the woman. Obviously influenced by Degas, the composition has an informality more usually associated with him; the vigorous brush-work, however, is typical of Renoir

Monet revived a suggestion made by the late Bazille as early as 1867 for an independent artists' exhibition. Early in 1874 Monet, Pissarro, Berthe Morisot, Renoir, Degas, Cézanne, Sisley and Guillaumin formed the "Société anonyme des artistes, peintres, sculpteurs et graveurs". A group exhibition was held at Nadar's photographic studio from April 15th to May 15th, 1874, in the Boulevard des Capucines. The exhibition aroused an unprecedented storm of abuse. Singling out Monet's study of the harbour at Le Havre, **Impression Sunrise** (see Plate XV), the journalist *Leroy* epitomized the general feeling when he dismissed the picture as the "impression of a painting". The name stuck; by common consent attacker and defender accepted the new title.

Manet however declined to exhibit with "these five or six lunatics, among them a woman", because he still felt that his destiny was to overcome the resistance of the Salon. From then on Monet was to be the dominant voice.

The following year, in March 1875, the Group organized an auction sale at the Hotel Drouot. This innovation proved yet another failure, the work of the Group being

(Above) **RENOIR La Yole**
This is a later development on the themes explored pre-war at La Grenouillère. Renoir weaves the same intricate patterns of dappled brush-strokes to suggest the movement and rippling of the water. It was painted during a period of financial difficulty. Later on, the days at Argenteuil seemed idyllic and were the most harmonious in the Group's existence

(Above) **MONET La Gare Saint-Lazare, Paris**
This picture, painted in 1877, coincides with the Third Impressionist Exhibition. Held in Rue Le Peletier, at premises rented by Caillebotte – an engineer and amateur painter whose patronage to some extent filled the gap left by the unfortunate Bazille – this picture was one of the major exhibits. Although the public reaction remained unchanged, Georges Rivière made sympathetic criticism of the exhibits. Monet painted several versions of this subject, steadily recording the scenes and events of everyday life in Paris

(Above) **RENOIR Luncheon of the boating party**
Throughout his life Renoir used his great ability to record scenes of everyday life around him. The Group seen here in 1881 in a riverside café, includes Gustave Caillebotte, the man in the foreground, an amateur painter and minor member of the impressionist Group, and Aline Charigot who sits playing with a puppy – she was shortly to become Renoir's wife

(Below) **SISLEY On the Cliffs**
All his life Sisley remained unswervingly devoted to the impressionist viewpoint. This canvas retains the atmosphere of the early days. Of all the Impressionists, fate was the unkindest to Sisley; he never attained recognition as a painter and, even today, is sometimes criticized on the grounds that he merely repeated, in later life, successful formulae of the past. His remarkable clarity of vision, though, is evident in this delightful canvas

received with derision, each bidder trying to submit a more absurd offer than the one before.

In April 1876 Durand-Ruel sponsored the Second Group Exhibition, at 11 Rue Le Peletier. This exhibition had only twenty participants as opposed to the thirty-six artists who had taken part in the first. The lesser academic artists who had been included at Degas' insistence in the former exhibition were now excluded. The significant additions were *Gustave Caillebotte*, an engineer who was an amateur painter, and the late Bazille, whose work was included in homage.

Once more the critics heaped abuse and ridicule on the exhibits claiming that the pictures were unfinished. But this time a small body including Castagnary, Rivière and Burty spoke up in support, and Duranty published his famous "La Nouvelle peinture", the first assessment of the Group as an entity.

(Above) **MONET Haystacks in the snow**
Monet was, by 1891, generally accepted as the greatest of the Impressionists and had acquired a ready market for his work. In that year, continuing his idea of working on series of pictures, Monet produced his **Haystacks** series. They were greeted by the public with enthusiasm but were regarded by the younger artists with some reservations, many feeling that they were slightly decadent concessions to Monet's love of colour, texture and light

(Above) **MONET Belle-Ile-en-Mer**
Moving to Giverny in 1883, Monet widened the range of his painting expeditions. In 1884 he worked at Étretat and, in 1886, he summered at Belle-Ile. He made many studies of the sea and surrounding cliffs and rocks, echoing the work done over twenty years previously at the Channel ports

(Right) **DEGAS Melancholy**
All his life Degas delighted in informal portrayals of young women. He had the ability to see them when they were least self-conscious and to record them faithfully, not from life but from recollection

The role played by Edgar Degas is always difficult to equate with the impressionist movement. Although he was inseparable from the Group, he was not really a member. Yet his caustic personality and ready sarcasm made him a formidable opponent in argument and, as a frequenter of the Café Guerbois, his lively wit and positive thinking illuminated the formative discussions of the Group.

Degas was logically the follower of classicism and, unlike the others, had been trained in the academic atmosphere at the École des Beaux-Arts in the class of Louis Lamothe, who had been a pupil of Ingres. A friend of Edouard Manet from early times, Degas at first painted Delacroix-like subjects; but he was determined to be original in conception, and the composition of his pictures was always daring. Like Courbet, he was able to dispense with stereotyped formulae and produce arrangements in his work which defied traditional approaches.

As early as 1870 he had decided never to exhibit again in the Salon, and was bitingly sarcastic when financial expedience forced Monet and others to submit work to the selection jury. Greatly influenced by Japanese art, Degas managed to juxtapose dark, almost silhouette forms, against low horizontals or contrasting verticals, often directing the subject's pose out of the picture, and returning

the beholder's attention to the focal point by the diagonal use of an article of furniture or similar item. He was fundamentally opposed to painting in the open air, once remarking, "You know what I think of painters who work in the open, if I were the government I would have a company of police watching out for men who paint landscapes from nature. Oh, I don't wish for anybody's death. I should be quite content with a little buckshot to begin with . . . Renoir, that's different, he can do what he likes."

Degas' real connexion with the Group lay in the wonderful series of studies he made of dancers and bathers. Often painting from memory, he firmly believed in what he called "the editing quality of the human mind". He believed that working from recollection enabled the artist to dispense with the unimportant and remember only the essential. He stated, "It is a transformation during which imagination collaborates with memory; you reproduce only what strikes the eye, that is to say, the necessary. Thus, one's recollections and inventions are freed from nature's tyranny."

He showed work in seven of the eight Group exhibitions, only declining to show in that of 1882 because of what he considered the unjust exclusion of some of his followers'

(Above) **CASSATT The Box**
Mary Cassatt, an American and a pupil of Degas, first
exhibited with the Group in 1879. She continued as an
active member and participated in three subsequent
exhibitions. She collected impressionist paintings herself
and, on her return to America, did much to popularize
their work, and assisted Durand-Ruel when he introduced
them there

(Right) **CÉZANNE The Card Players**
In this canvas, based on a Le Nain painting, Cézanne
has masterfully captured the atmosphere of country
people playing cards. There are five other versions of
this subject by Cézanne; this one is a remarkable character study

work, and a quarrel about the aptness of the title of the
exhibition. However, despite all his professed misanthropy,
he formed several very close friendships. He was instrumen-
tal in the introduction to the Group of the American *Mary
Cassatt* in 1879. He was also a friend of Berthe Morisot,
and from 1885 supported *Gauguin*'s membership, buying a
canvas from him at the auction sale in 1891.

Later he transferred to the Café de la Nouvelle-Athènes
where a table was always reserved for him and his friends.
He loyally supported the monthly impressionist dinners
and continued to be an articulate central figure. Later,
harassed by failing eyesight, he changed from oil-painting
to pastels, brilliantly combining them with water-colours.

Meanwhile in 1872 Cézanne had joined Pissarro at
Pontoise. At last accepting that this technique was un-
suitable for his romantic aspirations, Cézanne prepared to
adopt the impressionist method. The kindly Pissarro
guided him skilfully, and thirty years later Cézanne still
spoke of him in moving terms as "humble and colossal",
acknowledging him as a father figure, "a man to be counted
on for sound advice".

Musée du Louvre

(Left) CÉZANNE Bridge at Maincy
Previously incorrectly called "Bridge at Mennecy", this picture was in recent years identified as one Cézanne painted at Maincy in 1897. It was formerly owned by Père Tanguy, the artist's colour-man, whose portrait was painted by Van Gogh. It then passed into the possession of Victor Choquet, the Customs officer who was one of the earliest patrons of the Impressionists. The air of calm and tranquillity, and the screening action of the three branches, underline Cézanne's progress as a landscapist

All was not well, however, with the Group. By 1880 the Fifth Group Exhibition was organized, at 10 Rue des Pyramides. Pissarro included an amateur painter, Paul Gauguin, in the Group. The previous year Renoir, Cézanne, Sisley and Berthe Morisot had abstained from the Fourth Group Exhibition, submitting their work to the Salon instead. Renoir and Berthe Morisot were successful; but Sisley and Cézanne, on their rejection, retired from Parisian life, Sisley to Moret and Cézanne to Aix. Following Camille's early death, Monet had moved to Vétheuil in 1878. Thanks to the patronage of a wealthy publisher, *Georges Charpentier*, Renoir at this time began to obtain lucrative portrait commissions, but not without making some diplomatic concessions to his impressionist style.

Monet soon unleashed his wrath spitefully against Gauguin. He declared, "I am an impressionist . . . but I seldom see my fellow impressionists any more, male or female. The sanctuary has become a commonplace school, opening its doors to any old dauber who knocks." Zola withdrew his support also, sourly remarking that the absence of a natural leader was the reason for the Group's demise. The harmonious Argenteuil period was now over.

(Below) GAUGUIN The Seine at Pont d'Iena
Paul Gauguin initially painted only as a dilettante, and collected several canvases by members of the Group. His work at this time was described as "diluted Pissarro" and, in this picture, one can see clearly the influences of that admirable tutor. It was Gauguin's inclusion in the Fifth Impressionist Exhibition which caused Monet to remark caustically that the Group now opened its doors to any old dauber who knocked

Musée du Louvre

Courtauld Institute Galleries

(Right) MANET Bar at the Folies-Bergère

Manet's last great work; this canvas was received at the 1882 Salon in a very different mood from that which had greeted **Le Déjeuner** twenty years before. The criticism which previously, inevitably, had greeted his work relented. But Manet was now a dying man. Since 1880 ataxic paralysis had steadily incapacitated him; in 1883 gangrene set in and he died shortly after an operation to amputate a leg. At his funeral, Degas ironically remarked, "We did not know that he was such a great man." The recognition which had been denied him in his lifetime speedily followed. As early as 1884, a major retrospective exhibition was held at the École des Beaux-Arts

(Below) RENOIR The Seated Bather

Renoir's approach to the depiction of the female nude was quite different from that of Degas. Degas wished to paint the nude in the intimacy of the bath or bedroom. Renoir wished to paint her out of doors, alone with nature, naked in the sunlight

Courtesy of the Fogg Art Museum, Harvard University. Bequest-collection of Maurice Wertheim

The diplomatic Durand-Ruel needed all his tact and persuasive power to organize the Seventh Group Exhibition in 1882.

By Manet's death on April 30th, 1883, the rifts were clearly visible. His final picture, **Bar at the Folies-Bergère**, is a fitting tribute to his use of the impressionist technique and is considered by many to be his finest work. Successfully submitted to the Salon of 1882, it brought him some belated recognition, and his nomination for the Legion of Honour afforded him some comfort. This was followed by an almost wholly appreciative article by Albert Wolff, the "Le Figaro" critic, who had so bitterly attacked the Second Group exhibitors. Manet wrote to him, "Thank you for the kind things you said about my exhibits, but I should not be adverse to reading, whilst I am still alive, the wonderful article you will dedicate to me after my death." This was not prophetic. Manet had already felt symptoms of the ataxic paralysis which was shortly to kill him.

The final chapter on impressionism and the prelude to later events was fittingly written by Berthe Morisot. In 1886 she organized the Eighth, and last, Group Exhibition including most significantly the young *Georges Seurat,* whose scientific *divisionism* was to produce an irreparable rift in the movement.

From then on the original constituent members pursued their own ways. Living apart, Monet at Giverny, Pissarro at Éragny, Cézanne at Aix, Renoir at Cagnes, and Sisley at Saint-Mammès, they seldom saw one another. Strangely enough, except for Sisley, who was never free from financial difficulties, the Impressionists now enjoyed better times. The turning point had been the success of Durand-Ruel's impressionist exhibition in New York in 1886. In future the art dealer was able to ensure that the artists had a regular and appreciative market for their work. Before we trace their final destinies, we must now examine the main-stream events in Paris.

The year 1886 was as vital to the history of art as was 1874. As well as seeing the end of impressionism, it heralds the birth both of *neo-impressionism* and *symbolism*. During 1884–1885 Seurat had been working on a large scale composition ultimately titled **Sunday afternoon at La Grande Jatte**, which proved to be the most controversial attraction in the Eighth Group Exhibition. His ideas were to paint in tiny dot-like brush-strokes, which he called divisionism and which shortly graduated into *pointillism*.

His younger colleague, *Paul Signac*, summed up their ambitions in his manifesto: "To divide tones is to take advantage of all the benefits deriving from colour and harmony. Firstly by the optical mixture of pure pigments, secondly by the separation of the various elements, thirdly

(Above) **RENOIR Les Parapluies**
As he became more successful through the patronage of the publisher Georges Charpentier, Renoir gradually became dissatisfied with the disciplines he now felt the impressionist technique imposed on him. It was at this time he exclaimed, "I have drained impressionism dry." He developed a new approach, ceasing to work out of doors and employing a linear method, based on a pen and ink preparatory drawing. Several names have been coined to describe this interim style; his "dry period", his "harsh period" and his "Ingres period". Suffice it to say that, temporarily, he abandoned his painterly approach and concentrated on his skill as a draughtsman

(Left) **SEURAT**
Sunday afternoon at La Grande Jatte
Introduced to the Group by Pissarro, Seurat's approach to painting caused the irreparable split in the impressionist ranks. In this large picture he asks the beholder to participate physically in the optical mixture. The grass is stippled with blue, yellow and green dots, which when "processed" by the viewer's eye unite the two primary colours and the resultant secondary colour. Similarly, the shadows on the grass contain these three hues plus red as the complementary covering tone, in accordance with the divisionist theories

(Above) **MONET The Doges Palace**
From 1890 Monet embarked on painting a series of pictures on the same subject. His celebrated London series was painted between 1899 and 1905. In 1908, he visited Venice and produced a series of the canals and palaces there

(Above right) **MONET**
Houses of Parliament, London
Between 1900 and 1904 Monet painted 37 views of the Thames. Fascinated by the foggy distortions of light, he worked on three themes: Charing Cross Bridge, Waterloo Bridge, and the Houses of Parliament

(Below) **SIGNAC The Palace of the Popes, Avignon**
Seurat's early death meant that his theories could only be developed by students of his work and imitators. His most enthusiastic follower was Paul Signac, whose treatise on pointillism assured Seurat's fame for posterity. It was not until the twentieth century that Seurat's genius was completely recognized; a retrospective exhibition held in 1892 attracted little attention and no sales

by the balance of these elements and their proportions by contrast, gradation and irradiation, and lastly by the choice of a brush-stroke commensurate with the size of the canvas.''

They represented grass, for example, by a series of pointillist dots, made up by using the secondary colour initially, plus the formative primaries and the complementary colour (green, with blue and yellow, and red as the complementary colour). Thus they asked the beholder to participate in the optical mixture.

In June 1884, Seurat, Signac, Cross, Angrand and Dubois-Pillet founded the "Société des Artistes Indépendants", elected *Odilon Redon* their president and met weekly at the Café d'Orient or Café Marengo. On being introduced to Signac and Seurat, Pissarro took up the new method, and in time the pointillist style spread to Belgium, Holland and Italy. In France other artists, including *Toulouse-Lautrec, Van Gogh* and Pissarro's son, Lucien, worked with the style. Monet held himself aloof, however, dismissing the movement as "non-artistic". When one compares the new scientific method with his own **La Grenouillère** (see Plate XIV) technique it is amazing how slight is the difference in intention.

Following the publication of Rimbaud's "Illuminations", the poet Moréas, in "Le Figaro" on September 18th, 1886, proposed symbolism as "the only name capable of reasonably designating the present-day trend of the creative spirit in art". A plethora of small magazines, among them "La Pléiade", "Le Décadent" and "Le Symboliste", appeared at the same time.

It soon became evident that Seurat and Signac were working on different themes from those of the Symbolists. Strangely, the symbolist movement was initially linked with the Gauguin-dominated "Impressionist and Synthetist Group exhibition" at the Café Volpini in 1889, although the name "Impressionist" was only included in the title because of its revolutionary connotations. Strangely, because Gauguin's aims were totally divergent from the neo-Impressionists, he wrote at the time that they, the Symbolists, "were concerned merely with the eye and not with the mysterious midriff of the mind".

Seurat's **Sunday afternoon at La Grande Jatte** followed on from the contrast of tints he had achieved in his **Bathing at Asnières** (see Plate XXIV). This huge painting, finally completed in 1886, was exhibited in the Eighth Impressionist Exhibition of that year, where it was the focal point and principal attraction. Painted entirely in the studio it was nevertheless based on twenty drawings and thirty painted sketches done "plein air". It is interesting to note that most of these preliminaries were painted on the

The Tate Gallery, London

(Above) **MONET Poplars on the Epte**
Like the work of the mature Turner, Monet's late works became vehicles for the representation of light. The **Poplar** series was produced in 1895 and, as always, represents the subject seen under various conditions at different times of day

Stedelijk Museum, Amsterdam

(Left) **VAN GOGH The Potato Eaters**
This was Vincent's first masterpiece. After his failure in Borinage and his interlude as a tramp, he began to study painting seriously. This theme is clearly inspired by Millet's depictions of peasants, but has been interpreted from his own observations in the coal-fields. In a letter he said, "I have tried to make it clear that these people, eating their potatoes under the lamplight, have dug the earth with those very hands they have put in the dish, and so it speaks of manual labour: and how they have honestly earned their food."

(Above) SEURAT La Parade
The figures remain stilted and immobile, but the atmosphere engendered is striking. Seurat attempts here to render the curious effects of the newly invented gaslight

(Below) TOULOUSE-LAUTREC
Battle of Flowers, Nice
This, an early Lautrec, was drawn after a family holiday at Nice where he had frequently stayed to convalesce. The drawing is dashed off with great freedom, the movement of the coach and horses matching the light-hearted atmosphere of the promenade crowd. The driver is reminiscent of an earlier painting of his father with the coach-in-hand at Nice

(Right) SEURAT Courbevoie Bridge
Painted on the Seine banks with all the apparent atmosphere of the Argenteuil scenes, it is incredible how little in the technical – but how much in the emotional – content this painting varies from Monet's work. To the uninitiated, they might seem to be similar, as each is composed from tiny dots or blobs of paint, but Monet's "romantic impressionism" would not tolerate Seurat's "scientific impressionism". This medium-sized canvas comes midway between the large-scale compositions Seurat executed entirely in the studio, and the innumerable small sketches that he painted directly from nature

lids of cigar-boxes! The problems of optics and the analysis of light and colour are of dominant importance, and these coincide with the wider knowledge of light effects occasioned by the invention of photography. Thus the appeal of the viewpoint to artists was considerable. The public, needless to say, was flabbergasted.

When in March 1886, Durand-Ruel sailed to New York, he took Seurat's **Bathing at Asnières** among the 300 impressionist canvases. The last Impressionist Exhibition had been divided into what Pissarro called "*Romantic Impressionists*" and "*Scientific Impressionists*".

These Scientific Impressionists had considerable influence also on other members of the new élite in Paris. In 1887 Vincent Van Gogh eagerly embraced the new ideal, converting it to his own vision. In **The Restaurant** he uses pointillist brush-strokes, irregular when compared with those employed by Seurat, but dutifully combining red and green, orange and blue dashes, in accordance with the complementary colour theory. Henri de Toulouse-Lautrec used the pointillist technique in his picture of 1887 **The Countess of Toulouse-Lautrec**. This lively portrait of his mother combines his own spirited line with a

(Below) GAUGUIN The Vision after the Sermon

Gauguin was determined to find a situation where man could live in communication with nature, untainted by the commercialism of the nineteenth century. He rid himself of the encumbrance of his family and from 1886–1890 lived primarily in Brittany. It is here that his ideas on synthetism were crystallized. His intention was to reject naturalistic representation and to depict the emotion or mood of the subject. Reducing the elements in his picture to brilliant units of colour separated by black lines, as in cloisonné enamels, this is intended to be both abstracted and decorated, the syntheses of the intellectual processes which inspired them

(Above) SEURAT Le Chahut

When the Group dispersed, each to work entirely on his own, Seurat became the major figure in pointillism. Only Pissarro and Degas of the senior members of the Group continued to exhibit with the young men. The decorative and mannerist insistences in this picture clearly pave the way for the new art of the 1920s

(Below) SEURAT The Circus

The static quality of Seurat's figures has been eliminated. The clown and the equestrienne bound with life and movement, matched by the exciting colours of red, orange, yellow and blue. Seurat was clearly moving to new innovations when his life was cruelly cut short by meningitis at the age of thirty-two

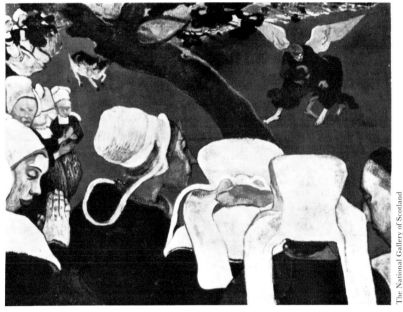

harmonious background of dabs and dashes in the divisionist mode. Even Gauguin toyed with the idea, but with characteristic crassness entitled the still life in this style **Ripipoint** or "dot and carry one".

Seurat's early death, on March 29th, 1891, at the age of thirty-two, halted fresh innovations. He had been arduously working on **Le Chahut** and **The Circus** both involving complex linear contrasts and patterns, anticipating many of the stylizations of the twentieth century. Signac took over the leadership of the Group and in 1899 published "From Eugène Delacroix to Neo-Impressionism", now considered an aesthetic classic, in which he outlined his theories on the principles of the movement.

Pissarro was by then feeling the restraints of pointillism which had at first given his art new impetus. Declining the offer of leadership on Seurat's death, he gradually reverted to a reinterpretation of well-trodden ways, finding at

(Above) **GAUGUIN Still Life with Puppies**
Deliberately distorting conventional ideas on perspective, Gauguin has tilted the table and dispensed with foreground and background. The puppies, the pears and the blue glasses appear equidistant from the viewer – emphasized by the decorative elements of the tablecloth, and each is treated with the same continuous black outline and two-dimensional form

(Right) **CÉZANNE La Montagne Sainte-Victoire**
Cézanne often painted this rugged, limestone mountain east of Aix. In his studies of the 3,000-foot peak, he reduces naturalism to a minimum. This, possibly the most successful study, owes much to the subtle angle of inclination of the tree-trunk and the frame created by the lateral bough

Éragny a retreat which stimulated him in his endless pursuit of the recording of light and nature.

It is appropriate here to mention Cézanne, who at this time was at loggerheads with each of the changes, and still considered strict adherence to nature the essential criterion. But the dominant voice must have been that of Gauguin. After his initial fascination with impressionism Gauguin gradually began to assume the leadership of the symbolist painters, as yet unnamed as such, in a reaction against naturalistic painting. Talks with *Émile Bernard* enabled him to combine his theories on simplification with a personal longing, to find a venue far removed from what he considered the tainting effects of urban civilization. Following a period in Britanny in 1886 and a brief sojourn in Martinique in 1887, which proved to be a significant indication of his eventual destiny, he returned to Pont-Aven in Finistère.

Gauguin combined anti-intellectual theories with a flat unrepresentational, almost childlike, decorative element; his **Still Life with Puppies** in 1888 presaged new horizons. Stemming from Bernard's *"cloisonnism"*, so named because the lines divided pictures into stained glass window like compartments as in cloisonné enamels, Gauguin's ideas on *synthetism* were born. From this inspiration younger artists including *Bonnard, Vuillard, Sérusier*

(Above) **VAN GOGH Vincent's bedroom at Arles**
About this picture Vincent wrote to his brother, Théo: "Colour alone has put the thing across, the simplification imparting a grander style to the work and hinting at rest and sleep generally. The sight of this picture is meant to relax the mind, or rather the imagination."

(Above) **VAN GOGH Self-portrait 1886–88**
In all, Van Gogh painted himself forty-three times. This picture clearly demonstrates his eager embracing of the pointillist style; but it is not a blind adoption of pointillism. Significant innovations have been made, particularly in the definite direction and the elongation of some of the brush-strokes

(Below) **GAUGUIN Van Gogh painting sunflowers**
In this, painted in 1888 during his ill-fated interlude at Arles, Gauguin captures in an uncanny way the unrest that was latent in him. "Vincent and I don't agree at all about painting . . . he admires Daumier, Daubigny and Rousseau . . . all people I can't abide, and loathes Ingres, Raphael and Degas, three painters whom I admire."

and *Maillol* founded the *"Nabis"*, an exhibiting group named after the Hebrew word for prophet.

While in Pont-Aven Gauguin kept in contact with Van Gogh who had left Paris for Arles in Provence, and by persistent solicitation Van Gogh persuaded him to join him there. On his arrival Gauguin was amazed to discover that the wild Dutchman he had known in Paris had invented for himself the ideal technical vehicle for his talent. It was an approach diametrically opposed to his own theories, and his ego refused to acknowledge the validity of Van Gogh's discoveries. The tragic outcome of their relationship is well known; suffice it to say that, as a result of the constant friction between the two, Gauguin fled back to Paris, leaving Van Gogh self-mutilated and mentally impaired.

Gauguin returned to Britanny and continued to work at Pont-Aven and Le Pouldu. In 1889 he painted **The Yellow Christ** (see Plate XXVIII), a milestone in his career, in which for the first time he achieved a completely satisfactory balance between emotion and objective vision.

71

Öffentliche Kunstsammlung, Basel

(Above) **GAUGUIN Ta Matete**
Gauguin determined to find "modern day ancient
Egyptians living naked under the sun"; the preconceptions manifest in that sentiment are obvious here. The
stilted poses he had seen in the Egyptian Rooms at the
Louvre are faithfully reproduced. Here, Gauguin is
essentially a European attempting to paint what he
thinks he ought to see; later he became totally identified
with the culture of Oceania, and combined this with the
decorative elements of Maori art which he had seen en
route in Auckland, New Zealand

From then on Gauguin began to direct his attention to the
tropics. He was fascinated by the Egyptology in the
Louvre and his ideas crystallized after seeing the Javanese
model village in the World Exhibition. In April 1891 he
set sail for Tahiti.

Spurred on by his idea of discovering "modern day
ancient Egyptians living naked under the sun", the
mannerism of **Ta Matete** is self-explanatory. He steeped
himself in native folklore, and glowing colours filled his
new canvases. His imaginative interpretations of Polynesian
life had been enriched by a visit he made en route to
Tahiti to the Maori Museum at Auckland in New
Zealand. However, beset by self-made difficulties, Gauguin's life pattern was always disturbed. Despite this, a
wonderful flow of masterpieces steadily emerged. His
initial uncertainty gave way to an unerring vision which
enabled him to capture the essence of native existence. In
1893 he was repatriated to France, destitute, but bringing
with him such fine canvases as **The Moon and the Earth**
and the **Spirit of the Dead keeps Vigil**.

His stay in France enabled him to reassess his attainments, and attempt to reorganize his finances to combat

(Right) **GAUGUIN**
 The Spirit of the Dead keeps Vigil
This picture dates from Gauguin's first Tahitian journey.
Returning to his hut one night, he found his house-girl in
a state of cataleptic paralysis, induced, he said later, by
fear – fear of the spirit of death who had passed by but
not taken her. He wrote, "the Kanakas think that the
phosphorescent glows of night come from the spirits of
the dead, they believe in them and fear them. I have made
a nude of a young girl . . . I put a little fear in her face. I
must provide a pretext for the fear . . . I have made the
ghost just a plain little woman, for the girl who has never
seen a French stage-ghost can only picture the spirit of
the dead as looking like the person who has died, in other
words a person like herself."

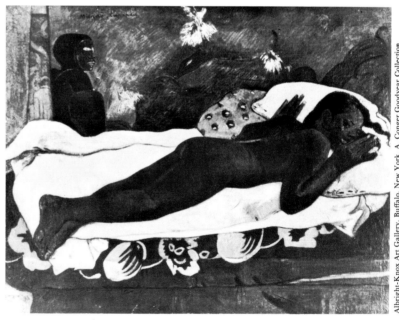

Albright-Knox Art Gallery, Buffalo, New York. A. Conger Goodyear Collection

the difficulties he had experienced on his first visit to the South Seas.

His persistence and determination became symbolic of the artist's struggle to find self expression even when faced by insufferable odds. Despite the theatrical elements visible in his external posturings, the internal anguish and the sacrifices were very real. Gauguin's eventual return to Oceania and his death there made him a legend. His impact on modern art is immeasurable.

When an attempt is made to assess objectively the achievements of Vincent Van Gogh, one is conscious of the thrill in itself of recounting his biography. Behind this dramatic story a similar aspiration exists, although in many ways his art is the antithesis of Gauguin's. His total contribution to the century is remarkable.

His arrival in Paris in 1886 marked the beginning of a new era. The impact impressionism made on him was considerable and, for the first time also in his life, apart from his intimacy with his younger brother Théo, his sense of personal isolation was removed by the comradeship of the cafés. He already had a knowledge of Japanese art, having avidly collected prints during his days in Ant-

(Above) **VAN GOGH La Guinguette**
Vincent painted this suburban café shortly after his arrival in Paris to join his brother Théo. He retains in this picture his sombre palette, but soon encountered three major sources of inspiration: Japanese prints (he had already in fact developed an interest in these), impressionism and pointillism

(Above) **VAN GOGH**
Sailing boats at Saintes-Maries-de-la-Mer
Seeing the fishing-boats on the beach, Van Gogh painted them to look like Japanese woodcuts. He wrote: "The Mediterranean has the colours of mackerel, changeable, I mean. You don't always know if it is green or violet, you can't even say if it's blue, because the next morning the changing light has taken on a tinge of rose colour or grey."

(Below) **GAUGUIN Under Pandanus**
Although this was painted during a period of trial and tribulation for Gauguin, his personal vision is now absolute. He successfully unites his European ideas, combined with knowledge based on a careful study of Japanese prints, with a "remote and savage" culture

(Above) **VAN GOGH The Sower**
Combining inspiration from both Japanese prints and
Millet's picture of the sower, Vincent's version has
immense dramatic power. He wrote of it: "I have had a
longing on me for such a long time to do a sower, but the
things I've wanted for a long time never come off." This
picture, a little over one foot high, is one of the most
effective Vincent produced at Arles

(Below) **VAN GOGH Old Peasant**
Van Gogh's finest portrait. He wrote to Théo: "You are
shortly to make the acquaintance of Master Patience
Escalier, a sort of 'man with a hoe', formerly cowherd
of the Camargue." The man with a hoe is a reference to
a famous Millet. Vincent organizes the radiating dabs
and dashes of paint in a masterly way, so that it possesses
almost the quality of a Byzantine mosaic

werp. His religious obsessions behind him, he began to
emerge from his Millet-dominated stylizations, and with
the advice of Pissarro, Lautrec and Degas he began to
achieve a harmony between impressionism and Japanese
art, amalgamated with the newly experienced pointillism.
He felt socially more secure then and bemoaned the passing
of the Barbizon colony, feeling that in such a haven he might
have found a niche for himself. A chance remark by
Lautrec sent him southwards to found an artists' colony.
Happening on Arles in Provence he worked with frenzy,
inspired by the light and colour; he lived alone, worked
exhausting hours, eating little and becoming more and
more introspective. The volume of work he produced at
this time is as yet unequalled in art history. Ordinary
everyday things and people became thrilling elements in
his compositions. The dabs and strokes of his brushes
fashioned patterns and movements hitherto undreamt of. A

(Above) **VAN GOGH Cottages at Cordeville**
Vincent joined Dr. Gachet at Auvers-sur-Oise. An admirer of contemporary painting, Dr. Gachet had long been an intimate of Courbet,
Manet, Pissarro and Cézanne. The violence within the artist manifests
itself in every line he paints; the cottages undulate and writhe with
serpentine lines; the grey sky moves with motions of its own. Throughout we are conscious of the conflicts which soon culminated in his self-
destruction

Courtesy of the Museum of Fine Arts, Boston. Gift of Robert Treat Paine

(Left) **VAN GOGH The postman Roulin**
In Arles Vincent became acquainted with the local post-man, Roulin. He admired his character, his strength, his unfailing good humour and his capacity for work; in all he painted him six times. He wrote: "I am now at work with another model, the postman in a blue uniform, trimmed with gold, a big, bearded face, very like Socrates."

(Below) **VAN GOGH Road with cypresses**
After his mental collapse, Vincent's painting became more dramatic. His skies began to reflect the emotional storms which were raging within him. His cypresses writhe with flame-like contortions, yet he described the cypress in tranquil terms. It was, he wrote, "beautiful in line and proportion like an Egyptian obelisk"

Kröller-Müller Stichting, Otterloo

change in his emotional balance permeates these pictures, communicating to the beholder his struggles and anxieties.

After the Gauguin interlude Van Gogh's work changed a great deal. Following the cataclysm of his first bout of insanity, he enjoyed periods of reason interrupted by frequent and violent seizures, during which he was unable to work. He was sustained only by the love and protection of his brother Théo during these crises, and was able to resume painting, calming himself in moments of tension by copying from Daumier, Delacroix, *Doré, Rembrandt* and his original favourite Millet.

His art passionately began to explore light, emotion and movement, gradually introducing those flame-like writhings which dominate **The Starry Night** (see Plate XXIX) and **Road with cypresses**. He was determined to return to the north and agreed to join Pissarro's friend, the amateur painter *Doctor Gachet,* for medically supervised residence at Auvers. His art became steadily more frenzied, he achieved serpentine contortions with the paint, and his draughtsmanship at times verged on the unrealistic. The drama and violence which now seems an inseparable part

(Above) **VAN GOGH Self-portrait with severed ear**
Here his mental and physical deterioration is brutally
apparent. He wrote, "I was thin, as pale as a ghost." But
it is far more than mere loss of weight that we notice here:
the resignation evident in his demeanour is matched by a
mortal hurt; his haunted eyes betray his misery

(Below) **TOULOUSE-LAUTREC**
Woman pulling up her stocking
An intimate study ranking with Degas' pastel nudes.
Dashed off like a snapshot, it is produced, like so many
of his best works, in oils on cardboard

of his personality is most obvious in his final work **Cornfield
with Crows** (see Plate XXX). His dying words, after the
clumsy and prolonged way in which he took his own life,
"there will never be an end to human misery", echo those
gloomy corridors of his mind.

The arrival of the talented amateur painter Henri de
Toulouse-Lautrec at *Léon Bonnat's* studio in March 1882
aroused little comment. This painter transferred to
Fernand Cormon's studio on Bonnat's retirement and stayed
there until 1886. A natural draughtsman, his work was to
some extent modelled on that of Monet and Degas. By 1885
he was an habitué of Montmartre, and his mis-shapen
figure was well known in night-life circles.

He shared an interest with Van Gogh in Japanese prints,
and during 1887 he exhibited with him at the cabaret
"Le Tabourin". He also met the young artist Pierre
Bonnard who had recently designed a lithographic poster
French Champagne. He introduced Lautrec to his
printer Ancourt, who explained the technical process. He
became friends with Aristide Bruant, the cabaret artist and
song-writer, and designed and executed a lithographic
poster for him. Continuing Bonnard's idea, Lautrec
proceeded to make revolutionary innovations in a formerly
non-artistic medium. He rapidly followed this with other

(Above) **GAUGUIN Nevermore**
The masterpiece of his second Tahitian stay, this splendid study shows
how utterly Gauguin has integrated himself into Polynesian life. He
had "reacted back beyond the Parthenon", beyond the "feeble
recreations of the Hellenic age". The simplifications are matched by
the accuracy with which he employs the minimum amount of model-
ling, to suggest form; without intruding into the realms of mere
representationalism

prints advertising the newly popular "Moulin Rouge" and artistes such as Jane Avril.

Lautrec also painted the scenes around him. With a natural penchant for depicting movement and atmosphere with a few economic strokes, he devised a personal approach of great originality. Because of his deformity, occasioned by breaking both legs as a child, he loved to sit strategically placed, paints at the ready, in the night-clubs of Paris. Using unprimed cardboard, he combined the neutral buff background as a design element in the pictures he produced and, using petrol-thinned paint, he deployed bold slashing strokes, areas of plain and stippled, almost pointillist, pigment to make eye-catching illustrations. From 1889 he became a regular exhibitor at the *Salon des Indépendants*.

Like Degas he was primarily concerned with the female figure, and in his pictures created an intimacy between sitter and artist rarely previously achieved. He immersed himself in the fringe existence of low-life Paris, frequenting and eventually living in the brothels of the Rue des Moulins. The *au salon* pictures explored a new dimension in art, covering a range of subject-matter hitherto considered improper. He had the supreme ability to record without striking a moral attitude. He made no distinction between projects. The same originality of approach covered

(Above) **GAUGUIN The Day of the God**
After his return to Paris in 1893, Gauguin felt less allegiance than ever to European society and painted Tahitian scenes from memory. This remarkable picture, painted after he had sustained a broken leg in a brawl, owes much to Hokusai's **The Wave** in his treatment of the sea in the background

(Above) **TOULOUSE-LAUTREC**
Mademoiselle Dihau playing the piano
Degas had already painted Désiré Dihau playing the bassoon, when Lautrec painted his sister at the keyboard

(Left) **TOULOUSE-LAUTREC Jane Avril poster**
Lautrec sketched the artists performing at the Ambassadeurs, the Jardin de Paris, the Eldorado and the Folies-Bergère. He was particularly attracted to Jane Avril, whose explosive dancing had earned her the nickname "Mélinite". Rejuvenating the art of poster design, Lautrec completed thirty-two posters in all and four hundred lithographs in only nine years

commercial illustration or formal painting subject.

However, his personal life was beginning to make vast inroads into his practical work. Never robust, the excesses he practised shattered his constitution. In 1899 he was confined in a sanatorium at Neuilly suffering from acute alcoholism. While an inmate he produced from memory a superb series of circus drawings, to prove to his father that, whatever his physical debilitation, his intellect was undulled. After his release he reverted to heavy drinking and died on September 9th, 1901, at Malromé.

The impact made by these three artists, Gauguin, Van Gogh and Lautrec, is naturally of enormous importance to any assessment of artistic progress in France during this period. In the final estimation however, the mature work of Paul Cézanne is the most significant contribution of all. Cézanne's recognition came most belatedly. Derided by the critics, Cézanne had been a consistent failure until his previously mentioned self-reappraisal under Pissarro's supervision.

(Above) **TOULOUSE-LAUTREC**
La Goulue – Moulin Rouge
Zidler, the director-founder of the Moulin Rouge, asked Lautrec to design a poster. At only 27, he produced this spirited design of La Goulue and Valentin-le-Désossé, the principal dancers. It typifies his skills and owes much to Japanese inspiration

(Below) **TOULOUSE-LAUTREC** **Marcelle**
Prostitute she may be, but Lautrec gives her dignity in his own way. With a few virile strokes of the brush, he brilliantly captures both the world-weariness of her face and her own innate simplicity

Musée Toulouse-Lautrec, Albi, France

(Above) **TOULOUSE-LAUTREC**
Chocolat dancing at Achilles Bar
After performing at the "Nouveau Cirque", Chocolat would visit Achilles Bar in the Rue Royale. Lautrec shows him here dancing and singing for a few habitués in an impromptu exhibition. The economy and skill of Lautrec's technique is brilliantly displayed here, each line and block of colour helping to build up the required atmosphere

78

Musée Toulouse-Lautrec, Albi, France

(Left) **TOULOUSE-LAUTREC**
Au salon de la Rue des Moulins
Lautrec lived and worked in the Paris brothels for four years; his revelations of that world are unique – scenes never before painted, yet without judging or embellishing. The Press described him as "leaving the trace of his curious evil genius, the talent of a deformed man who sees everything about him as ugly"; but he turned his eye to any subject, faithfully interpreting what he saw

Courtesy of the Museum of Fine Arts, Boston
Bequest of John T. Spaulding

(Above) **GAUGUIN Women with a white horse**
Hoping to find the native culture of the Marquesas Islands uncorrupted, Gauguin soon found himself in fresh trouble with the authorities; he drifted from one crisis to another, racked by illness. This picture may have in it premonitions of his death, for within a few weeks he was buried in the cemetery visible at the top of the canvas

(Below) **CÉZANNE Lac d'Annecy**
The theories Cézanne had successfully applied to still life were now directed to landscape painting. This beautiful picture, painted at Annecy, demonstrates the satisfactory transference of his vision

Courtauld Institute Galleries

He was dismayed by the progress of events in Paris and full of contempt for all kinds of "official" art. By 1886 he felt himself to be still completely misunderstood by critics and public alike. A man of enormous integrity, he at no time in his life made any concession to public taste or fashion. Cézanne was fortunately never completely deprived of faith in himself, although the hostility of the critics had an inhibiting effect on his personality.

The publication in 1886 of Emile Zola's "L'Œuvre" deeply wounded Cézanne, who sensed parallel between the novel's hero and himself, and it resulted in the ending of a life-long friendship. The death of his father, in the same year, removed an obstacle to regularizing his private life. He married Hortense Fiquet and legitimatized his son by this liaison. Now comfortably off, he lived in the family home at the Jas de Bouffan near Aix.

No artist has ever been more methodical than Cézanne. His work was exhaustively thorough in both preparation and execution. It is far removed from the passionate exuberance of Van Gogh or Gauguin. He once remarked that he looked at nature "until his eyes bled".

Gradually he began to evolve a new approach to art.

(Above) TOULOUSE-LAUTREC
Tête-à-tête supper
Painted with amazing vitality, the subject is a private party at Le Rat Mort in Rue Pigalle. Using a Degas-like composition, Lautrec slices through the man, the fruit-dish and the chandelier. His health had deteriorated through excessive drinking and he had been forced to spend three months in a clinic recovering from delirium tremens. Within two years he was to die, having reverted to alcohol on his release

(Below) POUSSIN Et in Arcadia ego
Cézanne greatly admired this picture and appreciated both its intellectual message and artistic skill. The message spoken by death is "Even in Arcadia there am I", but is usually rendered as "I too have lived in Arcadia", reflecting on the transience of human existence Cézanne said, "every time I see Poussin I know myself better . . ."

Using brush-work both as a means of emphasis for the structure and also as a surface decoration, he meticulously radiated his strokes. Although the difference in mood in his pictures suggests sometimes quiet and orderly applications, sometimes harsh and violent, in reality his work took months to finish. Spectators have recorded how sometimes there were intervals of up to twenty minutes between single brush-strokes.

Cézanne was animated by a confessed desire to "make Poussin live again according to nature", and began to experiment widely. Using a very narrow range of subject-matter he confined himself to still life, landscape and portrait painting. He carefully selected certain arrangements then repeated them over and over again, making infinitesimal alterations each time.

To enhance the reality of his painting and to enrich the surface area he evolved a geometric approach. Aiming "to represent nature by means of the cylinder, the sphere, the cone, all placed in perspective", he simplified the subject-

(Above) CÉZANNE House of the Hanged Man
The house, the last occupant of which had committed suicide, was at Auvers-sur-Oise, where Cézanne was painting after his stay with Pissarro. It was painted at a time when critics and public ridiculed his work. Using an impressionist technique, he had subjugated his romantic aspirations

matter initially into basic geometric shapes. Having sensed these forms he made them "according to nature", partially eliminating any instrusive contour.

This viewpoint was co-ordinated by his own decorative sensibility, and gives added presence whether to sky, tree-trunk, mountain, fold in drapery, fruit or vegetable. This simplification of form enabled him in his mature work to balance perfectly these constructional elements.

During this time he expanded his range of subject-matter to include figure compositions, known as "the bathers". With varying success he attempted here to apply his theories to his original love of the female figure. Mindful of local prejudices he did not employ models but relied on his life classes attended thirty years previously.

Imperceptibly his reputation grew. In 1889 *Victor Chocquet* had arranged for his **House of the Hanged Man** to be shown at the Paris World Exhibition. He was then invited to show in Brussels with "Les Vingts", a group of twentieth-century artists. Vollard, the art dealer, organized a one-man show for him in Paris in 1895 which amazed younger artists. In the Salon d'Automne of 1904 he successfully exhibited thirty-three paintings and felt himself utterly vindicated in the eyes of the critics. Afflicted by diabetes since 1890 his health began to fail. In 1906 he was caught out of doors, while sketching, by a violent storm. He collapsed soaked and, contracting pneumonia, died shortly after. In the Salon of 1907 fifty-six paintings were shown as a major retrospective exhibition.

Pablo Picasso in this year carried Cézanne's theories one stage further forward when in **Les Demoiselles d'Avignon** he combined semi-abstract compositions, negro sculptural influences and the nude form broken down into constituent planes, and in the final picture left untouched the constructional forms. From then on *cubism* was a recognized art form, but the vision was that of Cézanne.

In the aftermath of the Impressionists, the early twentieth century saw fresh generations of artists reacting with mounting violence against the impressionist viewpoint. It is, however, of interest to see how the original members worked in their final stages.

The unhappiest lot fell to Sisley. Never equipped to earn

Musée Toulouse-Lautrec, Albi, France

(Above) **TOULOUSE-LAUTREC La Modiste**
This lovely painting is unusual for Lautrec; painted in 1900, it is bathed in a soft, almost impressionist light. The sitter was Renée Vert, a mannequin and milliner, the mistress of a painter friend of Lautrec, Adolphe Albert

(Below) **CÉZANNE The Plaster Cupid**
At Aix-en-Provence, Cézanne abandoned the romanticism of his youth and painted from still life. He minutely examined the surface structures of commonplace domestic articles. Exploring their spatial relationships, he attempted to enhance his representationalism by building form based on geometric construction, then "blurred out" these shapes "according to nature"

Courtauld Institute Galleries

(Above) PISSARRO Self-portrait
It was Pissarro's diplomacy and indulgence that held the Group together for so long. He alone showed in all eight of the Exhibitions, and constantly injected new blood into the membership. During the late 1880s he adopted the pointillist technique, modifying it to harmonize with his own vision

(Below)   PISSARRO
Boulevard Montmartre at night
Painted from a window of the Hôtel de Russie in 1897, the canvas possesses great vivacity. Some of the pointillist virtuosity is retained; rapid dabs and strokes of brilliantly contrasted paint suggest the surging traffic and crowds

a living, he lived at Moret on the edge of the Fontainebleau Forest, isolated and neglected. He was constantly embarrassed by financial worries, and was never accorded the recognition he deserved. In 1899 he died, remaining faithful to the original conception of impressionism to the end. Critics have said that by constant repetition of well-tried exercises he dulled the spontaneous element in his work. I cannot completely agree with this. The pictures he painted on the Gower Peninsula in South Wales in 1897 are full of finesse, allied to delicious colours which defy the vicissitudes of time.

Pissarro died in 1903. Abandoning pointillism and avoiding symbolism, he reverted to painting from the numerous apartments he occupied. He worked in Le Havre, Dieppe, Rouen and Paris. A typical example is the beautiful **Boulevard Montmartre at night** 1897. The effect of rain and light reflects the atmosphere of bustle and involvement, the thronged cafés, the busy street, are sensed rather than depicted. He worked right up to the end of his life, and his final pictures still possess the vivacity of youth.

(Above) RENOIR Les Baigneuses
Renoir, although crippled by arthritis, worked at Cagnes to the end of his life. He painted in brilliant, iridescent colours, repeatedly depicting his favourite model, Gabrielle, in incandescent settings. When his cruelly distorted fingers could no longer hold his brushes, he had them strapped to his wrists

(Above) **CÉZANNE Les Grandes Baigneuses**
Remembering the life-classes of his student days, Cézanne repeatedly worked on nude studies from memory. This composition was unfinished despite seven years being spent on it. "This will be my picture, my legacy to the world," he said. Despite this enthusiasm and the monumentality of the figures, the painting fails to achieve the same presence that his arrangements of fruit and commonplace objects possessed

Berthe Morisot died young. She had, like Sisley, always kept faith with the original conception of impressionism, and with Pissarro she formed a dependable nucleus for the movement. She successfully combined her roles of artist and mother. She died at the age of 54 during the 1895 influenza epidemic.

Degas turned almost exclusively to painting the female nude in his later years. He was totally disinterested in the artificial atmosphere of the life class, nor did he see the subject in the same light as Renoir. He wished to show women in the intimacy of their bathroom or bedroom attending to their toilet. Using glowing colours and brilliantly informal sweeping brush-strokes he invented a new approach to the depiction of the nude. Like Pissarro and Monet his last years were clouded by encroaching blindness. As were other members of the Group, he was much influenced by the cult of painting groups or series of pictures, in his case mainly of dancers or nudes. He

(Above) **GAUGUIN Breton village under snow**
This nostalgic picture was the last Gauguin painted. Discovered in his studio at Hiva-Oa after his miserable death, it markedly contrasts with his tropical surroundings. Maybe he knew that the legendary Polynesian Black Ship, which heralds death, was shortly to call for him and his latest thoughts were of happier times

(Below) **DEGAS After the Bath**
Degas perfected a personal approach to picture-making. Employing a device he called pastel tempera, he mixed pastels with fixative and blended the preparatory stages in opaque layers. He finished the picture either by superimposing pastel strokes or by applying wash tints with a brush. As his eyesight deteriorated, he found this method easier to handle than oils

(Above) **MONET Le Bassin aux Nymphéas**
After 1883, Monet lived at Giverny, becoming more and more a recluse as he grew older. He had a pool in his garden specially constructed and made 48 pictures from the lilies growing on it. He wished, he said, to express "something impossible . . . in rippling waters with tall grass undulating in the sun"

(Below) **MONET Water-lilies** (detail)
The longest lived of the Impressionists, Monet died in 1926. His last works are controversial; to some they are decadent "the means becoming the end", to others "the Sistine Chapel of impressionism"

experimented with sculpture as his sight deteriorated, following on to his **Little Dancer**, shown in the sixth Impressionist Exhibition of 1887. This **Little Dancer** was made from wax and dressed in a muslin tutu. His later sculpture is modelled in massive form quite opposite to the subtle delicacy of this figure. Becoming more and more eccentric with advancing age, he died virtually blind in his beloved Paris in 1917.

Renoir's attainments in his declining years are superb. Following his harsh period of the early eighties, Renoir allowed his disciplined use of linear constructions to lapse, and returned to painting in the impressionist mode, enhancing his work with brilliant colour. This stage is usually called his Iridescent Period. As the remorseless encroachment of arthritis curtailed his movements he repeatedly sought the sun. By 1910 he had settled more or less permanently at Cagnes on the Riviera. Crippled by the disease his mind and vision were more alive than ever before and, forced to give up landscape painting, he turned like Degas to the female nude. Using his favourite model Gabrielle, he created magnificent, timeless versions of womanhood naked under the sun. Exulting in light and colour the mature nudes possess a matchless beauty. "Dried like a burnt stick", as he described himself, despite the most acute suffering he continued to paint, having the brushes strapped to his wrists, when he could no longer hold them. He died in 1919.

Despite the irony of an attempted suicide in 1867 Monet was the longest lived member of the group. Like Degas he became obsessed with painting sets of pictures, to emphasize his sensations. He experimented with cathedral façades, poppies, haystacks (as did Pissarro), poplars, floods, London bridges and finally water-lilies. Moving to Giverny, he constructed a pool by diverting the Epte through his garden. Between 1904 and 1908 he did a series of forty-eight canvases which Durand-Ruel exhibited in his gallery in 1909. Like the mature Turner, he virtually forsook naturalistic representation allowing his matchless technique to become a vehicle for his vision. He died an eccentric recluse in Giverny in 1926, by which time his once daring innovations had receded into history.

CHRONICLE OF EVENTS

1748   Birth of David

1767   Birth of Girodet

1771   Birth of Gros

1780   Birth of Ingres

1784   David, **Oath of the Horatii**

1789   Storming of the Bastille
David, **Lictors bringing to Brutus the bodies of his sons**

1791   Birth of Géricault

1793   Execution of Louis XVI; the Reign of Terror
David, **Marat assassinated**

1798   Birth of Delacroix

1801   Birth of Bonington
Girodet, **Ossian receiving the shades of French soldiers**

1804   Napoleon becomes Emperor of France

1807   Birth of Diaz

1808   Birth of Daumier
Gros, **Napoleon at the Battle of Eylau**

1812   David, **Napoleon in his study**

1814   Napoleon retired to Elba
Restoration of the Bourbons, Louis XVIII
Ingres, **La Grande Odalisque**

1815   Napoleon defeated at Waterloo. Restoration of the Bourbons

1817   Birth of Daubigny

1819   Birth of Chassériau and Jongkind
Géricault, **The Raft of the Medusa**

1821   Death of Napoleon

1824   Death of Louis XVIII. Charles X becomes king
Death of Géricault and Girodet. Birth of Boudin
Delacroix, **The Massacre at Chios**

1825   Death of David

1827   Delacroix, **The Death of Sardanapalus**

1828   Death of Bonington

1830   Revolution in France. Overthrow of Charles X
Louis-Philippe becomes king

1832   Birth of Manet
Daumier, **Gargantua**
Imprisonment of Daumier in Sainte-Pélagie
Ingres, **M. Bertin**

1834   Birth of Degas

1835   Death of Gros
Corot, **Avignon from Villeneuve**

1839   Birth of Cézanne

1840   Birth of Monet

1841   Birth of Berthe Morisot, Renoir, Bazille and Guillaumin

1845   Birth of Mary Cassatt

1848   Revolution in France. Louis-Philippe abdicates
The Second Republic established
Charles-Louis Bonaparte declared President
Birth of Caillebotte and Gauguin

1850   Millet, **The Sower**
Courbet, **The Burial at Ornans**

1851   Coup d'état. Charles-Louis Bonaparte seized power

1852   The Second Empire proclaimed
Bonaparte becomes Emperor Napoleon III

1853   Birth of Van Gogh

1855   Paris World Exhibition. Courbet's "Pavilion of Realism"
Courbet, **The Artist in his Studio**

1856   Death of Chassériau
Courbet, **Young girls on the banks of the Seine**

1857   Millet, **The Gleaners**

1858   Orsini bomb plot to assassinate Napoleon III

1859   Franco-Austrian war
Birth of Seurat
Pissarro and Monet at the Académie Suisse

1860   Monet in Algeria on military service

1861   French intervention in Mexico

1862   Bismark becomes Prussian Premier
Manet, **Concert at the Tuileries**
Monet, Sisley, Renoir and Bazille at Gleyre's studio

1863   Salon des Refusés. Manet, **Le Déjeuner sur l'herbe**
Ingres, **The Turkish Bath**
Monet, Sisley, Renoir and Bazille at Fontainebleau
Birth of Signac. Death of Delacroix

1864   Maxmilian crowned Emperor of Mexico
Fantin-Latour, **Hommage à Delacroix**
Bazille, Boudin, Jongkind and Monet at Honfleur
Birth of Toulouse-Lautrec

1865   Monet, **Olympia**
Monet, **Le Déjeuner sur l'herbe** at Chailly

1866   Seven Weeks War. Austria defeated by Prussia at Sadowa
Monet, **The Fifer**

1867   Maximilian executed in Mexico
Monet, **Women in the Garden**
Manet, **The Execution of Maxmilian**
Death of Baudelaire, Ingres and Théodore Rousseau

1868   Bazille, **The Family Reunion**

1869   Monet at the Café Guerbois. Pissarro at Louveciennes

1870	Franco-Prussian War. Defeat of Napoleon III Establishment of the Third Republic. Siege of Paris Manet, Degas, Renoir and Bazille in the army Bazille killed in action at Beaune-La-Rolande Cézanne at L'Éstaque Pissarro, Monet and Durand-Ruel in England
1871	The Commune. Destruction of the Vendôme Column Courbet in Sainte-Pélagie, then flees to Switzerland Corot, **The Belfry at Douai**
1872	Pissarro, Cézanne and Guillaumin at Pontoise Monet at Argenteuil, often visited by Renoir and Sisley
1873	Degas in New Orleans Sisley at Marly. Berthe Morisot at Mauricourt Cézanne, **House of the Hanged Man** Manet, **Le bon Bock**
1874	First Impressionist Exhibition, at Nadar's studio Caillebotte joins Monet, Manet, Renoir and Berthe Morisot at Argenteuil
1875	Auction sale at the Hotel Drouot Death of Corot and Millet Sisley, **Flood at Port Marly**
1876	Second Impressionist Exhibition Duranty, "La Nouvelle Peinture" Death of Diaz Monet, **Gare de St. Lazare** series Renoir, **Le Moulin de la Galette** Degas, **L'Absinthe**
1877	Third Impressionist Exhibition Van Gogh in the Borinage as a preacher Monet moves to Vétheuil
1878	Death of Daubigny
1879	Fourth Impressionist Exhibition Degas meets Mary Cassatt Renoir, **Madame Charpentier and her children** Death of Daumier and Monet's wife, Camille
1880	Fifth Impressionist Exhibition Disagreements within the Group
1881	Sixth Impressionist Exhibition Birth of Picasso
1882	Seventh Impressionist Exhibition Manet, **Bar at the Folies-Bergère**
1883	Death of Manet Renoir, **Les Parapluies** Gauguin with Pissarro at Rouen
1884	"Les Vingts" founded in Brussels
1885	Van Gogh, **The Potato Eaters**
1886	Eighth Impressionist Exhibition Durand-Ruel's Impressionist Exhibition in New York Gauguin at Pont-Aven. Van Gogh in Paris Seurat, **Sunday afternoon at La Grande Jatte** Zola, "L'Œuvre". Rimbaud, "Les Illuminations"
1887	Van Gogh and Toulouse-Lautrec adopt pointillism Gauguin in Martinique Cézanne, **La Montagne Sainte-Victoire**

1888	Seurat, **La Parade** Van Gogh in Arles, joined by Gauguin Van Gogh, **Sunflowers**
1889	Paris World Exhibition Van Gogh, **The Starry Night** Gauguin, **The Yellow Christ**
1890	Monet, **Haystacks** series Cézanne begins **The Card Players** series Van Gogh commits suicide at Auvers Monet moves to Giverny, constructs his water-garden
1891	Gauguin goes to Tahiti First Toulouse-Lautrec poster for the Moulin Rouge Death of Seurat, Jongkind and Rimbaud
1892	The "Nabis" Exhibition Monet marries Madame Hoschedé
1893	Monet begins **Rouen Cathedral** series Gauguin returns to France from Tahiti
1894	The Dreyfus affair Toulouse-Lautrec, **Au salon de la Rue des Moulins** Death of Caillebotte
1895	Gauguin returns to Tahiti Death of Berthe Morisot
1897	Impressionists' exhibition in London
1898	Gauguin, **Whence came we, what are we, whither go we?** Death of Boudin
1899	Signac, "From Delacroix to Neo-Impressionism" Renoir returns to Cagnes The "Nabis" at Durand-Ruel's Death of Sisley
1900	Paris World Fair. Centennial exhibition of French art Monet begins **Water-lilies** series
1901	Death of Toulouse-Lautrec
1902	Monet, **Waterloo Bridge** series Death of Zola
1903	Founding of the Salon d'Automne Death of Pissarro and Gauguin
1904	Renoir and Cézanne exhibit at the Salon d'Automne Death of Fantin-Latour
1905	Van Gogh and Seurat Exhibition Salon des Indépendants
1906	Salon d'Automne. Gauguin Exhibition Death of Cézanne
1914	Outbreak of World War I
1917	Death of Degas
1918	End of World War I
1919	Death of Renoir
1926	Death of Mary Cassatt and Monet
1927	Death of Guillaumin
1935	Death of Signac

GLOSSARY

Académie Suisse   Parisian school of painting attended by Pissarro – he met Monet there in 1859. Cézanne and Guillaumin also attended the school, which paralleled the Group gathered round Monet at Gleyre's as as one of the main sources of impressionism

atelier   studio, workshop (Fr.)

au salon   a euphemism for a brothel

barbes de bison   a word-play on the French for beard. The artists affected bison beards to accord with the wild, unkempt forest of Fontainebleau

Barbizon   a forest village near Fontainebleau which became the site of a colony of artists who painted from nature

Baudelaire, Charles Pierre   (1821–67) author, poet and critic, best known for his "Les Fleurs du Mal"; a friend of Courbet, Daumier, and Manet, who admired their work

Bazille, Frédéric   (1841–70) a member of Gleyre's academy. A prominent member of the group of young artists known as "Manet's gang", principally interested in painting figures out of doors

Bernard, Émile   (1868–1941) associated initially with Signac and pointillism, he met Gauguin in 1886 and helped evolve the cloisonnist style of painting

Bonapartism   the movement which supported the family made famous by Napoleon I and their cause, during the period 1815– 1851 until Charles-Louis Bonaparte became the Emperor Napoleon III in 1852

Bonington, Richard Parkes   (1801–28) an Englishman working in France. In 1820 he entered Baron Gros' studio where he met Delacroix. Famous for his Normandy and Picardy landscapes

Bonnard, Pierre   (1867–1947) a friend of Vuillard and a member of the "Nabis", who painted in a modified impressionist technique known later as intimism

Bonnat, Léon   (1833–1922) portrait painter and professor at the École des Beaux-Arts. Toulouse-Lautrec enrolled at his studio in 1882

Boudin, Eugène   (1824–98) worked mainly at the Channel ports where he painted seascapes "plein air". An important influence on Monet and the young Impressionists

Caillebotte, Gustave   (1848–94) an engineer and amateur painter who joined the impressionist Group during the Argenteuil period. To some extent he replaced Bazille in the role of patron as well as companion

Cassatt, Mary   (1845–1926) an American painter introduced to the impressionist Group. She exhibited in four of the Impressionist Exhibitions

Cézanne, Paul   (1839–1906) a schoolfriend of Émile Zola, he decided to become an artist and enrolled at the Académie Suisse in 1861. His wildly romantic style was consistently rejected by the Salon. After the Franco–Prussian war he exhibited in the First Impressionist Exhibition of 1874 where his work met a hostile Press. In 1873 he stayed at Pontoise and was taught the impressionist technique by Pissarro. After 1886 he concentrated on geometric constructions, looking for the cone, sphere and cylinder in nature. In 1895 his genius was beginning to be recognized and by 1900 he was entirely vindicated. The last years of his life were spent on numerous versions of **La Montagne Sainte-Victoire** and huge compositions of bathers in landscape settings

Charpentier, Georges   wealthy publisher, Renoir's patron

Chocquet, Victor   a Customs official who collected the

work of Delacroix, then that of Renoir and Cézanne. He was painted by both the latter and was one of the first people to recognize their genius

classicism the true definition is art derived from "antique" examples. It also means art of established excellence and that based on the style of the Italian High Renaissance

cloisonnism the style of painting evolved by Gauguin and Bernard at Pont-Aven in 1886. Its name was derived from its resemblance to cloisonné enamels, being strong, flat colours separated by bold contours not unlike the leads in stained glass windows

Commune literally, a group of people acting together for purposes of self-government. The Parisian insurrection of March 10th to May 29th, 1871, also goes by this name. Thiers' troops recaptured Paris from the "Central Committee", during which engagement more than 20,000 members of the first "workers' republic" perished

Constable, John (1776–1837) English landscape painter, who exhibited **The Hay Wain** in the 1824 Salon

Cormon, Fernand (1845–1924) a painter of portraits and historical subjects in whose studio Toulouse–Lautrec enrolled on Bonnat's retirement

Corot, Camille (1796–1875) one of the first artists to paint directly from nature, recording the hourly changes of light. He evolved a Salon style which earned him a comfortable living, but his work made directly from nature is free of the fuzzy poesy of his official art and was admired by Monet and associates

Courbet, Gustave (1819–77) rabidly anti-clerical and anti-intellectual, despite his friendship with Baudelaire, he soon became notorious. In his paintings he comments on abject poverty, rebelling against both classicism and romanticism. His **The Burial at Ornans** established him as a leading figure in the realist movement. He also painted frankly erotic nudes, but his delightful landscapes mark him as a precursor of impressionism. Despite bitter criticism his reputation grew, but his political involvement in the Commune forced him into exile in Switzerland, where he died in 1877

Crome, "Old" John (1768–1821) founder of the Norwich school of landscape painters with John Sell Cotman

cubism derived from Picasso and Braque carrying Cézanne's theories on geometric construction one stage further. Leaving the structural elements visible in the finished picture, they concentrated on spatial definition rather than naturalism

Daubigny, Charles François (1817–78) a landscape painter much influenced by the Barbizon school. With Corot, one of the first artists to record hourly changes of light

Daumier, Honoré (1808–79) a prolific lithographer and cartoonist. He painted numerous scenes of the Courts of Justice and faithfully recorded the life of the poor in Paris; using intense chiaroscuro, he anticipated the impressionist approach to light particularly in his Don Quixote studies

David, Jacques Louis (1748–1825) joined Vien's studio in 1766. In 1775 he went to Rome to concentrate on painting from the "antique". He eagerly embraced the ideals of the Revolution and, appointed to the Convention, he voted for the execution of the king. An extremist and an admirer of Robespierre, he later abandoned violent republicanism and became an ardent Bonapartist and first painter to the Emperor. His established standard of technical excellence became synonymous with neo-classicism

Decamps, Alexandre-Gabriel (1803–60) French, biblical painter, the most famous of the romantic orientalists

Degas, Edgar (1834–1917) initially he concentrated on historical pictures and portraits. He took part in the First Impressionist Exhibition, although never a true impressionist; his affinity with the movement stems from his "impressions" of ballet dancers and the female nude. His conception of painting the female nude marks him as one of the greatest innovators in art history. In later life, his eyesight deteriorating, he evolved a new technique of mixing oil-paints and pastels

Delacroix, Eugène (1798–1863) a distinguished classical scholar in his youth, he greatly admired Géricault. His **The Massacre at Chios** marked him as the logical successor to Géricault as leader of the younger school. He extended the range of subject-matter to include themes from history, literature and poetry; only one of his major canvases – **Liberty leading the People** – comments on contemporary events. Ingres' implacable opposition to his work made him a controversial figure. He ceased to exhibit at the Salon after 1859, discouraged by the critics' persistent attacks. He painted murals with success and is famous for those in the Luxembourg library, Saint-Sulpice church and the Hôtel de Ville

Diaz de la Peña, Narcisse-Virgile (1807–76) one of the major landscape painters at Barbizon. His "plein air" paintings show romantic traits, and he was considerably influenced by Delacroix

divisionism a theory and method of obtaining brighter secondary colours by using the formative primaries, and leaving the spectator to provide the "optical mixture". The term was used by the neo-Impressionists to describe their technique in preference to "pointillism"

Doré, Gustave (1832–83) a prolific romantic book-illustrator, who gained immense popularity

Durand-Ruel, Paul (1831–1922) the Parisian art dealer whose brave, staunch patronage eventually made the Impressionists famous. His major achievement was the American exhibition of 1886 which established the artists in a foreign market

École des Beaux-Arts painting academy in Paris which taught the "official attitude" towards the arts

Fantin-Latour, Théodore (1836–1904) painter of portrait groups, still life and flowers. Mainly remembered for his **The studio in the Batignolles** in which he depicts, among others, Manet, Bazille, Monet and Renoir

Fontainebleau Forest a royal hunting forest near Paris

Franco-Prussian war August 1st, 1870 to May 10th, 1871. Fought by France and Germany; ostensibly caused by the Hohenzollern claim to the Spanish throne. The war was continued after Napoleon's capture at Sedan by the 3rd Republic, but after the seige of Paris the French capitulated and peace was signed

Gachet, Dr. Paul (1828–1909) an amateur painter and collector of impressionist paintings. A particular friend of Cézanne, Pissarro and, later, Van Gogh

Gauguin, Paul (1848–1903) after a period in the Merchant Navy and then as a stockbroker, he became an amateur painter. Much influenced by Pissarro, he also collected works of Manet, Cézanne, Monet and Sisley. He exhibited in the Fifth Impressionist Exhibition in 1880, and in 1883 decided to become a full-time painter. He lived in poverty in Paris and moved to Pont-Aven in 1886. His work there with Émile Bernard was chiefly responsible for the evolvement of synthetism. In 1887 he visited Martinique after working as a labourer on the Panama Canal, and in 1888 wintered at Arles with Van Gogh. The next year he produced his first masterpiece, **The Yellow Christ.** Two years later he went to Tahiti to paint according to his vision. After a brief visit to Paris he returned to Tahiti in

1895, and a period of intense personal suffering ensued. Desperately ill, he attempted suicide, painting his epitaph **Whence came we, what are we, whither go we?** After a series of incidents with the authorities he moved to the Marquesas Is. in 1901. Throughout his troubles he continued to produce outstanding canvases. Again desperately sick, his personal troubles worsened; sentenced to prison for assaulting an official he appealed to Paris, but died before the matter was resolved

Gautier, Théophile (1811–72) French poet, novelist and critic; an intimate of Manet

Géricault, Théodore (1791–1824) as a young man he exhibited **The Mounted Officer of the Guard** at the 1812 Salon, which gained him considerable fame. After 1817 he became the acknowledged leader of the romantic school of painters. His love of horses is reflected in many of his paintings

Giorgione da Castelfranco (1478–1510) a Venetian painter and pupil of Giovanni Bellini. His innovations had considerable influence on the development of High Renaissance art, particularly that of Titian

Girodet de Roussy-Trioson, Anne-Louis (1767–1824) originally a pupil of David, he gradually adopted a freer romantic technique

Gleyre, Marc-Gabriel the director of Gleyre's academy, a liberal school of painting in Paris attended at one time or another by such notables as Whistler, Manet, Bazille, Sisley and Renoir

Goya y Lucientes, Francisco José (1746–1828) the great Spanish painter whose mature technique shows him as a precursor of impressionism. He became a court painter to Charles IV, then a mysterious illness made him totally deaf and changed his personality. He recorded impartially the cruelties of the Peninsular War with his terrifying **Disasters of War** engravings. Later in life he produced nightmarish paintings of demons and witches

Gros, Baron Jean-Antoine (1771–1835) a pupil of David and major exponent of large pictures extolling Napoleon. On David's death he became the acknowledged leader of the classicist school

Guillaumin, Armand (1841–1927) a minor member of the impressionist Group. An amateur painter who became a full-time artist in 1892

impressionism essentially concerned with the depiction of light, with emphasis on painting out of doors

Impressionists, the name given to a group of artists originating in the Independent Artists Exhibition of 1874. Eight exhibitions were held under their name – in 1874, 1876, 1877, 1879, 1880, 1881, 1882 and 1886. The main participants were Monet, Renoir, Pissarro, Sisley, Bazille (posthumously), Degas, Berthe Morisot, Guillaumin, Caillebotte and Mary Cassatt. Boudin, Manet and Cézanne were also closely associated with the movement. The introduction to the **Group** of the work of Gauguin and Seurat caused dissensions which brought about the end of their exhibitions

Ingres, Jean-Auguste Dominique (1780–1867) a pupil of David, he earned a living as a portrait painter. He then worked in Rome for 18 years. Like his master David, he concentrated his studies on the "antique" figure, and perfected his technique. Later he became the undeniable leader of the classical school in Paris and the arbiter of good taste at the Salon. He enjoyed great success but his followers could not carry on his excellent technique. Although he experimented with romantic subject-matter his academic draughtsmanship continued to be of paramount importance

Jacobin an extreme radical. The word is derived from an extreme democratic club founded in Paris in 1789 near the Dominican convent of Saint Jacques

Jongkind, Johann Barthold (1819–91) a Dutch landscape painter who worked at the Channel ports in the 1860s. An associate of Boudin, he was a precursor of impressionism and considerably influenced Monet. A drunken Bohemian, he was one of the first artists to frequent Montmartre. He died insane

Legion of Honour French order of distinction created by Napoleon I, in 1805, to reward civil and military service

Leroy, Louis journalist on "Le Charivari", a satirical magazine. His mocking review of the exhibition in Nadar's studio in 1874 coined the term "impressionist"

lithographic of lithography. The process of drawing on stone and printing therefrom was invented by Alois Senefelder. It relies upon the affinity of grease for Bavarian limestone, and the rejection of water by grease, enabling the artist to print directly from a suitable stone. The technique has been developed in recent years by photography.

Louis XVI (1754–93) king of France; married Marie-Antoinette. A well-meaning but ineffectual man, he was overthrown by the Revolution of 1789 and executed in 1793

Louis-Philippe (1773–1850) king of France, nicknamed the "Citizen King"

Luxembourg royal palace in Paris built by Marie de Médicis. Under the 3rd Republic it was occupied by the Senate

Maillol, Aristide (1861–1944) French sculptor whose works are almost exclusively devoted to the female nude represented in a static and monumental way. At one time a member of the "Nabis"

Malmaison 17th-century château at Rueil-Malmaison. It was the home of the Empress Joséphine after her divorce

Manet, Édouard (1832–83) enrolled at Couture's studio from 1850–56. His exhibit was rejected by the Salon in 1859, but in 1861 he won a medal for his **Spanish Musician.** His **Le Déjeuner sur l'herbe** caused a scandal when exhibited in 1863, as did his **Olympia**

in 1855 and **The Fifer** in 1856. However, the younger artists acclaimed him enthusiastically. In the 1870s the hostility of the Press abated and Manet thought of the Salon as the proper venue for his work. Won over to the impressionist technique by Berthe Morisot, he painted in that mode from 1872 onwards. His studio gradually became the meeting place for society, but his health was deteriorating. In 1882 he began his last great work **Bar at the Folies-Bergère.** Although he was the perfect academic painter he was never recognized as such by the establishment and was denied, in his lifetime, the recognition he longed for

Maupassant, Guy de (1850–93) French writer of realistic novels and short stories

Millet, Jean François (1814–75) earned a paltry living as an artist from 1840 onwards, in 1849 moving to Barbizon. Although he painted from nature his ideals differed from the other artists there. He wished to portray the dignity of peasants in communication with nature – never forgetting his own humble origins. At first his work was dismissed as too realistic but by the 1860s he had a considerable following

Monet, Claude (1840–1926) introduced to landscape painting by Boudin, he later met Jongkind, Corot, Courbet and Daubigny at Le Havre. In Paris he enrolled at Gleyre's where he met Bazille, Renoir and Sisley, and then turned to painting "plein air" at Chailly. From 1869 he and Renoir worked together at La Grenouillère. In 1870 he fled to London where he met Durand-Ruel, and, after a trip to Holland, settled at Argenteuil for his most harmonious period. By 1883 some success enabled him to move to Giverny from where he travelled widely. He concentrated on series, painting cathedral façades, haystacks, poplars and finally London bridges and water-lilies

Morisot, Berthe	(1841–95) a pupil of Corot, she exhibited in all but one of the Impressionist Exhibitions and has a lively style not unlike that of Renoir during the Argenteuil period. Probably the greatest woman artist of all time
"Nabis", the	derived from the Hebrew word for prophet; the name was adopted by Vuillard and Maillol for a small group of artists working from 1889 to 1899 on the lines formulated by Gauguin and Maurice Denis in Brittany during 1889
Nadar, Felix	(1820–1910) an early photographer in whose studio the First Impressionist Exhibition was held in April–May, 1874
Napoleon I, Bonaparte	(1769–1821) a Corsican soldier who rose from obscurity to become General, 1st Consul, then Emperor of France (1804–15). The greatest soldier of the age, his policy of territorial expansion proved his personal talent but did not ultimately benefit the 1st Empire. His political reforms, however, were not only beneficial to France but to the whole world
Napoleon III, Charles-Louis-Napoleon Bonaparte	(1808–73) Emperor of France 1852–70, following his presidency of the 2nd Republic 1848–51
neo-classical	of neo-classicism; after the style of classical artists
neo-impressionism	strictly this movement has little to do with impressionism; in its purest form it is concerned with Seurat's divisionism, as expressed by his canvas **Bathing at Asnières**
New Republic	proclaimed after the overthrow of the monarchy, on September 22nd, 1792 – the first day of year 1 of the Republic
"odalisque"	an eastern female slave or concubine
œuvre	the total output of an artist or school of art
Ossian	legendary hero of Celtic mythology
Picasso, Pablo	(1881–1973) a most prolific artist. He experimented with Cézanne's use of constructional form, in **Les Demoiselles d'Avignon**, for example, developing them to cubism
Pissarro, Camille	(1830–1903) enrolled at the École des Beaux-Arts in 1855. Later he moved to the Académie Suisse where he met Monet, Guillaumin and Cézanne. Initially basing his work on Corot, he became a leading figure among the younger artists. He alone exhibited in all eight Impressionist Exhibitions, guided Cézanne's painting in 1872, and introduced Gauguin to the Group in 1880, and Seurat and Signac in 1885. He adopted the pointillist technique himself but later abandoned it
"plein air"	open air (Fr.); used to describe painting directly from nature, out of doors
pointillism	the technique of juxtaposing small strokes of pure colours on the canvas (see also *divisionism*)
Prud'hon, Pierre-Paul	(1758–1823) French artist unaffected by neo-classicism who continued to work in the style of Boucher doing portraits and large interior decorations
Quixote, Don	the almost blind knight and tragicomic hero from Cervantes' novel of the same name
Raimondi, Marcantonio	(c. 1480–1534) Italian engraver who was dedicated to the reproduction of important works by his predecessors and contemporaries. His engravings are now the sole surviving records of some lost masterpieces
Raphael	(Raffaello Santi, 1483–1520) one of the three great creators of the High Renaissance; a pupil of Perugino. In 1514 he became architect of St. Peter's, Rome. Famous for his Madonnas and his frescoes in the Vatican
Redon, Odilon	(1840–1916) leader of the Symbolists. He produced semi-impressionist vases of flowers and landscapes, and highly imaginative dreams, visions and nightmares
Rembrandt, van Rijn	(1606–69) great Dutch master whose daring brush-work and dramatic use of

	chiaroscuro anticipated the 19th-century romanticists		was championed by the critic W. Bürger (Thoré)
Renoir, Pierre-Auguste	(1841–1919) enrolled at Gleyre's and met Monet, Sisley and Bazille there. He worked in the Fontainebleau Forest in 1866, but despite the support of Corot and Daubigny his work was rejected by the Salon. He worked closely with Monet, painting at La Grenouillère. When the Group regathered at Argenteuil after the war he continued this association. He exhibited in the First Impressionist Exhibition and also in the disastrous auction at the Hotel Drouot. With Charpentier as his patron, his market grew, and from 1881 he withdrew from the Group and showed only at the Salon. In 1899 he moved to Cagnes and, despite increasing arthritis, he continued to work with the brushes strapped to his wrists	Ruisdael, Jacob van	(1628–82) Dutch painter whose landscapes, with their romantic element, greatly influenced European scenic art
		Salon	the original Salon exhibitions were held in the Salon d'Apollon of the Louvre, which gave rise to the name. The exhibition was an annual one after the Revolution, biennial before
		Salon des Indépendants	society founded in 1884 by Seurat and other artists rejected by the Salon
		"Scientific Impressionists"	a division suggested by Pissarro to separate the work of Seurat and his fellows from traditional impressionism
		Sérusier, Paul	(1864–1927) French symbolist painter closely associated with Gauguin, Maurice Denis and the Pont-Aven school
Robespierre, Maximilien Marie Isidoire de	(1758–94) instigated the Reign of Terror. Called "incorruptible", he was an implacable opponent of the Girondins, and was guillotined by the counter-movement to the Revolution	Seurat, Georges	(1859–91) entering the École des Beaux-Arts in 1878, he concentrated on drawing. Then he developed a technique incorporating small dabs of paint and glowing shades – known as divisionism. In 1886 Pissarro introduced him to the Eighth Impressionist Exhibition where his work caused a sensation
"Romantic Impressionists"	a division suggested by Pissarro to separate the artists working in the traditional impressionist manner from the new approach of Seurat etc., at the Eighth Impressionist Exhibition		
romanticism	fostered in France, like classicism, by the Revolution, it was demonstrated initially in the work of Géricault and Delacroix. The theatrical attitudes struck are mainly concerned with the enlargement of the range of subject-matter, and also with a relaxation of technique and a dramatic use of brush-work. The romantic emotions associated with drama and horror spread even to landscapes which often reflected human qualities	Signac, Paul	(1863–1935) Seurat's main follower; he wrote a dissertation on divisionism entitled "From Delacroix to Neo-Impressionism". He painted in the pointillist style but his work is considered an imitation rather than a development of Seurat's theories
		Sisley, Alfred	(1839–99) enrolled at Gleyre's in 1862, at which time he was able to paint in a dilettante fashion. Friend of Renoir, Monet and Bazille, he painted in the Fontainebleau Forest and frequented the Café Guerbois. Impoverished by the war he painted full-time from 1872 around Paris. He showed regularly at the Impressionist Exhibitions and also participated in the auction sale at the Hotel Drouot. Although never successful in his lifetime, he remained true to
Rousseau, Théodore	(1812–67) leading painter of the Barbizon school. Influenced by Constable, he worked directly from nature. His submissions to the Salon were rejected from 1836–48 until he		

impressionism but retained a personal originality

symbolism the name suggested by Moréas to describe the art, inspired by Rimbaud's "Illuminations", concerned with the rejection of realistic depiction in favour of the portrayal of things of the mind. Synonymous with synthetism, it concerned mainly Gauguin and the Pont-Aven artists

synthetism (see *symbolism*)

Talleyrand-Périgord, Charles Maurice de (1754–1838) a famous French statesman, and Minister of Foreign Affairs under Napoleon despite his emigré background. He negotiated on behalf of France at the Congress of Vienna

Titian (Tiziano Vecelli, 1487–1576) the great Venetian painter whose art paralleled that of Michelangelo in Florence

Toulouse-Lautrec, Henri de (1864–1901) was an infant prodigy as an artist. Deformed as a result of breaking both legs as a child, he enrolled at the École des Beaux-Arts in Paris in 1882. He was first at Bonnat's studio and then at Cormon's. Living in Montmartre he immersed himself in its night-life, and produced posters in the Japanese style of cabaret artistes and dancers. He greatly admired Manet's work; also inspired by Degas, he wished to paint the female nude in natural surroundings – the bath or the bedroom. He produced innumerable "au salon" drawings and sketches. Suffering from alcoholism, he spent some time in a clinic in 1899 and, although released, never really recovered

Turner, Joseph Mallord William (1775–1851) English romantic artist whose depiction of light anticipated impressionism. His work was known to Pissarro and Monet in 1870, the former describing Turner's approach as "tinted steam"

Van Gogh, Vincent (1853–90) early in life wished to be a theologian but, denied the opportunity, he became a tramp and, in 1882, an artist. He was inspired by Millet and by contact with miners in the Borinage. He followed his brother Théo to Paris in 1886, and there encountered impressionism, pointillism and Japanese art. He met Gauguin and Toulouse-Lautrec and, in 1888, moved to Arles in an attempt to found a congenial refuge for artists. He produced landscapes, portraits and flower pieces in bright colours heightened by passionate expressions of light and emotion. Following Gauguin's disastrous visit he mutilated himself by cutting off his ear. At times violently insane, he had periods of lucidity. His art became characterized by writhing flame-like forms, and grew steadily more emotional, matching the mounting crisis in his own life. He shot himself in the abdomen and, spurning aid, died two days later at Auvers

Versailles built by Louis XIV, the royal residence from 1681; the most elaborate palace in France

Vuillard, Édouard (1868–1940) French painter, friend of Bonnard and member of the "Nabis"

Waterloo the decisive battle of the Napoleonic war fought near Brussels on June 18th, 1815, it was Napoleon's final defeat and led to the overthrow of the 1st Empire

Whistler, James Abbott McNeill (1834–1903) an American working in England and France, who associated with Courbet and Manet. Mainly noted for the Japanese influences on his art and his use of musical sub-titles for his pictures

Wordsworthian the declared intention of William Wordsworth to express himself in the "language of low and rustic life" exactly parallels in literature the attitude of Millet in painting

Zola, Émile Édouard (1840–1902) French novelist, who defended Manet and his followers in numerous critical appreciations

INDEX